You are not the sum total
of your financial woes. You are a person,
who, among other things, has money dysfunction —
permanent but possible to recover from.
The feeling of ground glass in your stomach
you awaken with every morning can be removed by
making a commitment to recovery from
this shame-producing condition —
credit, cash and co-dependency.

Yvonne Kaye

Credit, Cash And Co-dependency

The Money Connection

Yvonne Kaye, Ph.D.

Illustrations by Daniel Sean Kaye

Health Communications, Inc.
Deerfield Beach, Florida

Yvonne Kaye, Ph.D.
22 North York Road
Willow Grove, PA 19090
(215) 659-7110

Library of Congress Cataloging-in-Publication Data

Kaye, Yvonne
    Credit, cash and co-dependency: The money connection/
Yvonne Kaye: illustrations, Daniel Sean Kaye.
      p. cm.
    Includes bibliographical references.
    ISBN 1-55874-133-X
    1. Codependents — Mental health. 2. Compulsive shopping.
3. Codependents — Rehabilitation. I. Title.
RC569.5.C63K39 1991   90-22709
616.85'227 — dc20   CIP

©1991 Yvonne Kaye
ISBN 1-55874-133-X

Publisher: Health Communications, Inc.
              3201 S.W. 15th Street
              Deerfield Beach, Florida 33442-8190

Cover design by Iris T. Slones

Dedication

I dedicate this book to my children:
   Rosanne Bowers
   Michelle Falbo
   Colin Kaye
   Daniel Kaye
   I love you.
For loving, unconditional support:
   Jane Drury
   John Aar
   Paula Roberts
   Dorothy Stephens
   Sister Mary Daniels, Dominican Retreat House in
      Elkins Park
   Marie Stilkind, Health Communications

   Kay Fogg — in loving memoriam

   To all those who have shared with me:
   Thank you — with love and gratitude.

                                          — Yvonne Kaye

I Spend. Therefore I Am.

Contents

.

Preface

Over the past years, I have presented at many varied meetings. Without exception, someone has come up to me afterwards and said, "I know you are talking about your own life, but you told my story."

It is important to note the similarity of the stories from all of us who come from dysfunctional families. Each person and history related here has been disguised, with names and locations changed. The information I have accrued over the past 35 years has come from people I have met all over the world. Even though a story might seem to describe a person you know, it applies to many of us. I have not yet heard one story that is unique to one situation or person. There is frequent repetition. In some cases, the examples given are a compilation of several people with similar circumstances. They identify no one. I have taken particular care to disguise the stories of people who are well-known. So if you think you recognize someone from my accounts, you are probably wrong. My hope is instead that you relate to the example and the suggested recovery process and find them helpful.

It is important for all people in any kind of recovery to know that their experiences with their families of origin, external family and other assorted big people were *their* experiences. I understand how other people from dysfunctional families lived and survived. I don't know how they feel. I only know for certain how I felt and how I feel today.

It is natural for others who knew the significant people in your life in their own special way to feel that your reactions are wrong. However, your reactions are to your unique situation. There is no right or wrong, good or bad — there just "is."

In his excellent book, *Same House, Different Homes*, Robert Ackerman (Health Communications, 1988) examines the varied aspects children of dysfunction see in their families of origin. Recovery means examining the facts as you understood them, not deciding whose perspective was "right" or who was to blame.

Remember, your recovery from whatever ails you depends on the rigorous honesty of your memory and the willingness to reverse the survival decisions you made as a young child. Those decisions have brought you much grief — it's time for a change.

One survival decision that is important for many of us to deal with involves money. Have you ever had friends who consistently forgot their wallets when you were eating out? What did you do? Paid for both meals, I'm sure. What else could you have done? Is your stomach constricting at the thought of confronting this habitual "forgetfulness?" Then, dearie, you are a cash co-dependent.

Yvonne Kaye

Introduction

- Mary Lincoln bought 300 pairs of gloves at a time.
- Imelda Marcos had more shoes than closet space.
- Jack L. had to buy the house next door to accommodate his hoarding. He's ready to move again.
- Heather P. died because she refused to spend money on a doctor.
- Frank J. sat in front of the television all day long after sustaining a serious injury. He only watched the stock trading channel. He made a lot of money — and lost his family.

These are only a few examples of the bizarre love/hate affair so many of us have with money. When did it all begin?

Inside every compulsive spender lives a quiet little child who knows that the best way to be loved is to steal pennies from Mother's purse and buy candy for the kids in the class.

In writing about compulsive spending, I feel a bit like a substitute teacher who was trained to teach French and has to teach math, which has always been her weakest subject. Compulsive and emotional spending is something I've suffered with unknowingly for years. There is much denial involved with money and spending issues. A great deal of it begins in childhood.

As will be seen in the following chapters, attitudes toward money are learned. Part of the conditioning process is that we stay within our family's status area. These attitudes undermine our adventuresome natures to pursue, take risks and — God help us all — be different. This book will explore the damage resulting from the dysfunctional attitudes toward money many of us have learned.

Money problems can cause embarrassment, shame, rage, guilt, confusion, suicide and homicide. They contribute to the stress responsible for such physical illnesses as hypertension, intestinal disorders and migraine headaches.

You want stress? Try the following:

- When the bills are more than cash in hand — and will be for a while to come.
- When you earn good money and wonder where it went.
- When the IRS just doesn't understand that you didn't understand!

Josephine's Story

Josephine knew this stress. Tall, slender and beautiful, she was also articulate and well-informed. When she walked into a room, people literally stopped their conversations to look. She would float from group to group, lightly touching an arm, a hand, a shoulder — complimenting men and women alike. She was the very essence of graciousness, assurance and charm. In spite of her appearance, even those normally threatened by such perfection liked her. She had it all — handsome husband, exceptionally attractive children and business acumen.

What has this story to do with money? Josephine was broke. Her self-esteem was the pits. She literally hated herself. She would weep in my office and say, "I don't know what is wrong — I know I'm good. I make a presentation to a corporation and they seem to really like me, but I don't get the contract. Why is that?"

Josephine taught business employees self-esteem, assertiveness and self-confidence. She would tell them, "If you imagine it, it will happen." She taught them well, overlooking her own discrepancies in the area of self-caring.

Low self-esteem is incredibly subtle. It eats away at self-preservation and emanates through one's aura to be recognized by others. Josephine's electromagnetic field said, "I'm not worth it," and that's why the contracts never came through. In addition, Josephine could get all the free presentations she wanted but they put her deeper and deeper into denial and fantasy. If you don't charge a fee, you are wonderful.

Josephine has stayed on the breadline as confused messages from her childhood continue to assail her. She just doesn't get it yet. She hasn't connected with the negative messages she received growing up. In addition to all this inner death, she is a perfectionist, hiding the problems of her family — that perfect family. Her terror mounts at the possibility that disaster might one day be uncovered. Someone might see the pain of not only today's looking-good family, but her family of origin who taught her she was worthless.

Does money make you happy? No — not in and of itself. When one's happiness is dependent on anything — a person, circumstance or thing — outside of oneself, it can be taken away and everything lost. External life, with money or anything else, is insecure. However, if you work on your own recovery to become happy with yourself, then money can help to increase your horizons. A happy, healthy person can have happy, healthy monetary habits. It isn't the mere possessions that cause the contentment; it is knowing who is in control.

In *Credit, Cash And Co-dependency*, there is much to learn.

Chapter 1

Credit, Cash
And Co-dependency

I was raised in a poor family. As I wrote that sentence I suddenly had a vision of people who thought they knew my nuclear family quite intimately saying, "What is she talking about? Poor? I suppose this is just another *Mommie Dearest* book. I never saw them going without food, clothing or shelter."

Only I knew what went on for me in my house — I really couldn't call it a home — and only I will ever truly know. The other two sides of the triangle I called my family are long since dead. There is still a fundamental loyalty in me that says I don't have to expose that much of childhood.

I really have had much difficulty in recalling a lot of my childhood, at least up until the past five years or so. I do know for sure that it wasn't good. I was an only child, living among a transient population of roomers, foster children and refugees. As the story unfolds it is apparent that money was a severe and continuing issue. So those people — including the extended family — who thought they knew my mother, my father and me, are going to wonder and probably end up believing this is a distorted way of being in the limelight.

They will just have to believe what they believe. I only know that sharing my perception of the way it really was is important to my recovery and may be helpful to yours.

Poor Relations

My mother was one of 13 children born to Polish immigrant parents in England. She was right bang in the middle and a raging co-dependent. She took care of everybody, younger and older. We were the poor relations. Until the age of 21 I thought, but hoped I was wrong, that her husband — who was erratic, bullying, intimidating and downright nasty — was my father. On my 21st birthday he informed me otherwise, which to some extent explained his behavior toward my mother. Out of nowhere he would tell her to get back to the streets where she belonged. I could never understand that one. Or he would say, "If you think I don't give you enough money, you know where you can earn it — with the other whores!" It wasn't exactly a healthy atmosphere for a small child who understood words but not meanings, who felt the emotions and ran from them.

Because of all these off-beat messages, I learned at an early age not to trust people with money. In my own external family, I found the wealthy relatives to be condescending. My mother was completely different in the company of her wealthier siblings, almost obsequious. She was the "go-fer" for all of them, handling large shopping bags, buying goods that were hard to come by during the war years and delivering them to her family. And all this on public buses.

There was absolutely no respect for my mother. One of her brothers would sometimes drop in for lunch — always bringing his own food because he wasn't sure if what we had was hygienic.

I would wear my cousin's hand-me-downs even though she was bigger than I was. When I was beginning to develop, I wore one of her bras — probably a 36C. I only had nipples. I felt such shame — I wasn't even good enough to fill her bra. Oh, the pain of puberty! I believe this is where the shame became so strong. I wasn't good enough even to wear hand-me-downs. I was a complete misfit.

Things were very bad when I was little, in every way. My parents and I had to move in with one of her sisters temporarily. It was a nightmare — probably for everybody. I only remember what I remember.

My beloved grandfather had died at that time, and my aunt had his magnificent rolltop desk in her house. I adored that desk. Somehow it brought me closer to the only man I had ever trusted. (When he died, my self-esteem died with him. I later discovered in my case it was merely comatose.) After my aunt's death during the later part of the war, I returned to that house, which had been partially bombed. My friend Jill and I broke in to find the desk missing. I went home and burst into the house, crying hysterically that Grandpa's desk had gone and that I now knew how my aunt "got rich."

That's how my 11-year-old mind worked. If you had money, you had to be bad, ruthless and evil. Because I was born on the wrong side of the tracks, I had no time for people who had money. To me money was associated with wickedness and would never ever bring any good. That was my first conditioning thought.

The Co-dependent Cycle Of Poverty

How horribly co-dependent children will distort their own roles in these dysfunctional families. They take re-

sponsibility for everything that goes wrong in their sur-
roundings, becoming overcompensatory little adults to
remedy the discomfort. How do these little adults try to
improve matters? In many cases they exchange roles with
their parents. In some cases they actually become the pro-
viders for the family by working, stealing, shoplifting —
whatever it takes to deal with the basics. Being co-dependent by default, they continue to express themselves in the
same manner as they grow into their chronological adult
lives by doing, giving and buying. This is their frame of
reference. This is how they learn survival, escape, approval
— and let's not forget — manipulation, lying and cheating.

People say it's better to be rich and miserable than poor
and miserable. That might be so. Impoverished people's
lack of sustenance puts them in a lower socio-economic
structure and that equals *shame*. See how the cycle becomes vicious?

Poverty	+ misery	=	shame
Shame	+ low self-esteem	=	lack of potential
	Lack of potential	=	poverty

How very sad! The mind-set is that, having been afflicted with these conditions, it simply isn't worth bother-
ing. "We'll never get out of this mess!"

Those who have it have been known to expound,
"Money won't change anything." *Wrong!* Being able to pay
one's bills, have an outing now and then, buy some clothing and save *make a difference*. However, for real change,
many messages received both verbally and behaviorally
from the past have to be rechanneled. Just recognizing
that attitudinal changes have to be made doesn't do it.

This book is about people who have severe financial
difficulties. Usually that statement speaks of insufficiency.
However, "not enough" is only one of a multitude of
guises. Some others are:

- Overspending
- Underspending
- Hoarding

- Inherited wealth
- Compensating
- Buying love
- Buying security
- Gambling for excitement

Some conditions are obvious; others just the opposite. From the street people carrying meager belongings in bags to the rock star who earns notoriety and declares bankruptcy, there is the common denominator of the "mystery of money." There you see it — there you don't.

The Masks Of Success

All this co-dependent behavior is to hide the pain of inadequacy, real or imagined. It is essential to understand that there is a vast difference between *being* inadequate and *feeling* inadequate. Unfortunately, the hidden compulsive spender doesn't know the difference.

The masks of success can be lethal. I have studied many professional people, women in particular. Many of them share the problem of low self-esteem. Many buy people, the same way I did in the past. I deal with plenty of bright, attractive, intelligent women, who on the outside look as if they have it all together. People look and say, "Boy, I wish I were like you. I wish I had it all together like you. You don't have any problems you can't deal with, do you?"

Watch for that looking-good stuff! It can maim you for life, if you don't seek what is beneath the veneer.

Dr. Maxwell Maltz, in his fascinating book *Live and Be Free Through Psycho-Cybernetics*, tells of his work as a cosmetic surgeon. He discovered that making people physically beautiful through surgery rarely changed their dispositions. His remarkable works on psycho-cybernetics (self-steering) address the need for the external to reflect the internal. We all know the internal needs attention!

Janice's Story

Janice was the wife of a very successful professional man. Her children were talented and genuinely charming.

Janice's co-dependency was outrageous. Not only was everybody else more important, but she didn't exist in her own eyes at all. She decided she wanted cosmetic surgery and that would take care of any problem.

Truly, there was very little discontent in her nuclear family. They all adored her. She felt safe with them. It was her family of origin and her association with them that caused the upheaval. She catered to them to the point that her husband and children requested an intervention. When I arrived, they had assembled surrounding Janice, who was in shock. "I don't understand all this," she said. "All I want is a simple face lift and the family goes wild."

What Janice did not understand was that her family was able to see the pain beneath her physical appearance. They told me many stories of how their mother had spoken strongly of breaking away from her siblings who took advantage of her. In many ways the similarity between my mother and Janice amazed me. The only difference was that Janice had wealth and my mother didn't. She would take to heart any statement, observation or criticism of her siblings. It would almost destroy her — and she saw buying for others as a way out.

Janice was an excellent hostess and would throw lavish parties, which were well-attended and a lot of fun — except for Janice. She was good at what she did as long as it showed "the best" for the guests. However, when it came to family celebrations, the level of stress increased 100 percent. One older brother and sister in particular wanted to be involved with her and her family.

The brother was a nervous man who created and appeared to enjoy scenes. He was never placed at the right table. The table was never set in the right position. The menu was not sufficiently balanced. The band was too loud. He could have done so much better with the money involved. And so on and so on.

The sister was incredibly jealous of Janice. She was a perfectionist and completely in denial in regard to her own devastating family situation. Her sons were both in terrible trouble with the law. One daughter was an underachiever.

But everyone was *fine*. Whenever Janice arranged a family party, she would be terrified and overcompensate. Everything had to be better than, finer than, cost more money than whatever had been done in the past. There was a genuine fear of criticism. Whatever she did, she never felt satisfied because of this family situation.

Then came her desire to have this work done on her face. Her nuclear family explained to me they were afraid she was doing this just to prove something else to her family of origin. Her family loved her as she was. We talked about that and Janice admitted it to me. Her daughter's wedding was coming up and she wanted to look spectacular.

Having studied Maxwell Maltz, I believed this was just another attempt to feel secure in the presence of her family of origin. As lovely as the wedding would be, as beautiful as her gown would be, she would not outshine her daughter. That was not her desire. But she felt having the jowls removed and the lines removed above the lip and along the eyes was something that would change matters with her brother and sister. Needless to say, I agreed with the family. Surprising Janice, I didn't necessarily agree that what she wanted to do was wrong.

She agreed to see me for a few sessions. We talked about the pros and cons of cosmetic surgery. My philosophy was, "You've got to get everything else in perspective." What I meant by that was that whatever she did, she could not change her brother and sister. When she learned to accept and live with that, if she still wanted the cosmetic surgery, then right on!

Janice was delighted with this but also afraid that she would not be able to accomplish the emotional detachment necessary. I believe what clinched the deal was my statement to her: "What if you have all these youthful looks about you and your feelings are still the same? What's next?"

We made a list of how she had survived the past in this family of origin, and every item we discussed had money attached. Her security in the marriage was due to the fact that there was plenty of money and no questions asked. If she had an argument with this brother or sister, she would immediately buy a gift or send flowers. At one time she sent her brother on a cruise. If any of the children graduated she sent an outrageously expensive gift or an enormous amount of money. Whenever she bought anything for herself, and her sister or brother would look at it askance, she would make excuses because there was so much guilt.

Beneath all that guilt, we discovered, was the fact that her mother had favored this particular brother and sister. She had demanded of their father a great deal of money to give them the best of everything — but the money wasn't there. So Janice had built up this identity of never believing she had a right to enjoy the money brought to her in her marriage. Her mother's attitude toward these siblings had infiltrated her mind and, after her mother's death, she felt she was responsible for their well-being. This meant guilt with a capital "G."

What I had to do with Janice was differentiate between guilt and shame. The shame she had inherited was that she was not worthwhile. Everything the family had in terms of money went to these two children. If anything was left, then Janice and her other siblings received some minimal benefit. As a consequence, she really didn't know how to handle having money in abundance.

As a result of her therapy, Janice decided to have the cosmetic surgery but halved her original request.

She attended her daughter's wedding looking just slightly younger but the same lovely woman that she is. The only difference this time was that Janice knew it. Money was no longer an issue. Her brother and sister came to the wedding and behaved in the same old way. Janice simply went on to another set of friends to make sure they were enjoying themselves.

To resort to another childhood teaching: "Money is the root of all evil." The actual quote, conveniently forgotten, is, "The *love* of money is the root of all evil." That changes things, doesn't it? If it isn't treated with knowledge, understanding and respect, like any other substance, money can control a person's very existence. "Knowing your worth" can take on a whole new meaning.

Never Enough To Feel Safe

One of the most helpful aspects of this kind of book, I believe, is to share one's personal experiences. What has been fascinating is how much has been revealed to me in the writing. Things I had not forgotten exactly, but not thought about have emerged.

Almost everything in our house was rented when I was growing up. I think we owned some of the furniture, but the house itself was rented, as was the oven, the heaters, even the tea kettle. There was never enough money to feel safe. Somehow, as much as the stringent wartime rationing would allow, we ate pretty well. My father and mother were both obese, and I recall the food being largely starch. Rarely was there salad. My mother had once owned a deli in an outdoor market in Brixton, South London, so she really knew how to bargain shop. It was always a terrible embarrassment to me when she would haggle.

In 1963 my former husband and I owned a small confectionery store in London. My mother, then a widow left with nothing but debt, worked there. Like most young parents, I raided her pantry when I visited, with her blessing. Her finances were chaotic but we were not aware of the extent of the problem. Even in those days my finances were chaotic, but we didn't confide in one another. That didn't happen in *our* family. So we played the game until November 12, 1963, when everything changed.

I drove to this tiny candy store to pick up the money for banking. My mother was waiting for me. As I got behind the counter with her, she opened the cash register and we were stuck! She was a large woman and I was seven months pregnant. We howled with laughter, released ourselves by shutting the drawer and went our separate ways. Four hours later, she was dead — at age 60.

What has this to do with money? The nightmare started the next day. We had been called to the house, made the arrangements and gone home to see to our two children and ask the neighbors to care for them for the next couple of days.

I was raised in a strictly Orthodox Jewish family. (Another myth laid to rest — not only are there Jewish alcoholics and drug addicts, but there are poor Jews too.) At that time I followed my religion, although I do not today. Women would come to a house to wash the body of the dead person, place her in the coffin and stay with her day and night until the burial. In the Jewish religion, the dead are never to be left alone.

Imagine my horror when I arrived back at the house early the next morning to discover that the electric company had disconnected the electricity because my mother hadn't paid the bill. There I was, seven months pregnant in a dark house, with my mother's dead body lying in her bed upstairs waiting for the women to come and prepare her.

I believe today that I was close to insanity at that point. In my hysteria, I screamed at her, "How could you do this? How could you be so stupid? Why did you have to die now?" I continued to cry and beat the walls, finally sinking to the floor in utter defeat. Frantic, terrified, vulnerable and confused, I was grateful that at least the telephone was still in order. (They turned that off the next day.) After a while I regained some composure and called the electric company. I told them the situation and asked what could be done. "Nothing," I was told, "until the bill is paid."

I had no cash to pay the bill and because of her reputation they refused a check. The banks weren't open yet. And I lost it. I screamed, "She's lying dead upstairs. Come around and see for yourself. What am I supposed to do — drag her body to your office to show you?"

I think of that time today and the tears flow — not with sorrow, but of rage against that kind of insensitive bureaucracy. Certainly in my rational state of mind, I know she did not pay the bill and the company didn't know she had died so they did what they had to do. After they were told, the attitude astounded me. "Well, she was in arrears and it's just too bad," threw me into frustration beyond belief. I told them, "There's no hot water to bathe her — the kettle is electric so I can't even heat any water that way." My pleas fell on deaf ears. Finally, I got in the car and drove to the electric company choking with tears and consumed with outrage, threatening mayhem if something wasn't done. The manager took my check and sent out a man — whom I invited to view my dead mother, which he declined. The power was restored in time for the women (who were already there, so I couldn't avoid the shame) to do their lovework. I call it that because it is considered a mitzvah (a blessing) in the Jewish religion to volunteer such a service.

What amazes me in retrospect is that until only a few years ago I had learned *nothing* from that incident and the power and my own telephone were disconnected on many occasions because of nonpayment. The entire insanity of that was that I had the money to pay. I just didn't do it. On reflection, I believe I internalized the rage to the point that I cut off my nose to spite my face.

"Let 'em wait for their money!" was the revenge that backfired.

After my mother's death we found envelopes and bags stuffed with unpaid bills and reminder notices. I never did that. I just left them unopened or filed them in the wastepaper basket. Is it genetic or environmental? Who the hell knows? I don't and I lived it for most of my life.

The co-dependency of this entire fiasco called "my mother's life" is that she spent so much money on everybody else outside of our nuclear family that she had none for her own survival needs. The facade, ignoring and hiding the fact of having insufficient funds, was just too much for my mother. I believe she died from co-dependency; whether from too many pills, a broken heart or simply despair, I'll never know.

Today I don't live like that. And when I die, everything will be in order — even my funeral.

Living one day at a time has helped me so much with this. That event with my mother's death was excruciating. After the incident, at her coffin, I was told not to cry because it would hurt the baby I was carrying. I didn't cry for her, for me or for the situation for another ten years.

This was part of my conditioning over money. Having recognized it as such, we can be deconditioned and reconditioned into a healthier monetary lifestyle.

Chapter | **2**

The Facts And
The Connection

I receive mail credit offers on an average of four times a month. Pre-approved, no-hassle, raised increments, they offer all the spice to enhance one's dream of wealth and glory. "Easy credit" is an eye-catcher, as are the tantalizing free trips, cars, microwaves and shopping sprees. They usually neglect to mention the need to pay for all this. The most prestigious establishments — banks, businesses and sometimes even the government — are involved in this kind of risk.

The government is even high on the list for gambling. State lotteries are responsible for many people involved in overspending for *the impossible dream*. Just look at the lines of people when the lottery winnings hit $20 million or so. People take second mortgages on their homes to buy thousands of tickets for the event — hardly healthy behavior.

Co-dependent people are caught up in the use of money and possessions as a way out of their problems. On a subconscious basis the messages are clear: "After what you have gone through, you deserve to have the best." Regardless of what you have gone through or even if you have had a very good life, of course you deserve the best. However, there is a small problem here. You have to be able to cover the cost of whatever you want to have. The self-esteem is so battered by the time the dysfunctionally raised child reaches maturity that any conflict can send it off on an amends-buying spree.

When I was a teenager, if I had an argument with a friend, I would immediately buy a gift to make it all better. I would never allow feelings to happen — I couldn't control my own, let alone anyone else's. Having someone angry at me would be alarming and I'd have to buy them off.

Most people in the United States, Canada and Europe are living well beyond their means. The United States government, the Parent Body, is doing the same.

It is estimated that the government has borrowed approximately $20,000 for each family of four. This figure comes in the nature of a warning from Harvard University economist Benjamin Friedman. He states that ". . . the average American family has enjoyed a higher standard of living since 1981 because of this loan." Payment is due now, so changes will have to be made in that standard of living. The Parent Government is also living on credit. What an example!

That means co-dependents must re-evaluate their spending habits, recognize their pain and find another solution. So far all that has been done has been to replace one agony with another — co-dependent mysteries with solid cash or credit.

In our culture we are encouraged to spend, spend, spend. Look at the TV commercials. Look at the billboards. Whichever way we turn, we are being coerced into spending what we don't have. It is extremely easy for someone with a weakened self-esteem to fall into this addictive pattern. People are constantly offered second mortgages or cash, with each company more accommodating than the last.

The commercials constantly lie regarding money. "Automobile rebates" — off what? The full price or what you can haggle down? "Easier to get loans!" "Easier than banks!" Sure, but how high is the interest rate? They don't mention that aspect, only the instant gratification — *and we fall for it every time.*

When I came to the United States from England and saw the credit cards here, I couldn't believe it. England wasn't like that back in 1968. It certainly is now. Interest rates on consumer loans is now often more than 25 percent. The United Kingdom certainly follows the USA in most things and this is no exception. The debt ratio has gone from 64 percent in the 1970s to 85 percent in the 1980s.

At that time, however, I did not realize how insidious the whole thing was. Being uncomfortable with oneself and being handed that piece of plastic is the same thing as handing an addict a needle, a pill or a drink. Insidious — that's the "in" word in terms of money problems.

The following is a questionnaire I used as a basis for some information for this book. When you have completed the answers, take a long look at the results. Then share them with a trusted person. There's a possibility that the denial is so deep you won't recognize a problem alone.

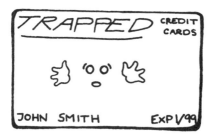

You And Your Money:
Self-Analysis Questionnaire

Your History: *Sex:* Male/Female   *Age:* _____

Circle or write in the correct answers.

1. Were you raised by two parents?   Yes   No

2. If not, with which parent did you live?
   Mother   Father

3. Did you live with another family member?
   Grandparent   Aunt/Uncle   Other _____

4. Were you adopted?   Yes   No

5. How many siblings?   1-3   4-6   7-15

6. Where were you in birth order? _____

7. Did you live in the:
   city   suburbs   small town   country

8. Did your father work?   Yes   No

9. What was your father's work? _____

10. Did your mother work?   Yes   No

11. What was your mother's work? _____

12. What kind of income did the family receive?
    Up to $6,000 per year $36,000 to $50,000
    $6,000 to $12,000 $50,000 to $75,000
    $12,000 to $24,000   Over $75,000
    $24,000 to $36,000

13. As a child did you know the family
    income?   Yes   No

14. Did you have your own bedroom?   Yes   No
    If not, with how many did you share and with
    whom? _____

15. Did you have your own television/
    telephone/computer?   Yes   No

16. What level of education did you complete?
    high school   junior college
    college/university   graduate school

17. At what age did you have a car? _____

18. Who bought it? _____

19. At what age did you have your first credit card?

    _____

20. How did you get it?
    Personal application   Parents   Friends

21. When you ran short of money to whom did you go?
    Mother   Father   Other _____

22. Did you pay for your own
    education?   Yes   No

23. Did you have a job while in college?   Yes   No

24. Did you have a savings account?   Yes   No

25. Was money ever discussed in your
    home as a child?   Yes   No

26. Was money an issue between your
    parents?   Yes   No
    a. Were there fights or arguments?   Yes   No
    b. What was the basis of the problems?

27. Was either of your parents an over-
    spender/underspender?   Yes   No

28. If you couldn't get money from either parent, to
    whom did you turn? _____

29. Did you ever go without:
    a. Food   Yes   No
    b. Clothing   Yes   No
    c. Shelter   Yes   No

30. Was there family involvement in the following?
    a. Mealtimes   Yes   No

b. Vacations	Yes	No
c. Discussion	Yes	No
d. Staying home together	Yes	No
e. Movies	Yes	No

31. Were you compared to other children? Yes No

Your Present:

32. Do you exaggerate your:

a. Income	Yes	No
b. Position at work	Yes	No
c. Family fortune	Yes	No
d. Family misfortune	Yes	No

33. Are you: Married   Single   Separated   Divorced

34. How do you earn your living?
    a. Human Services
    b. Medical
    c. Legal
    d. Commerce
    e. Outdoor
    f. Law Enforcement
    g. Architectural/Interior Design
    h. Education
    i. Physical Training/Instruction
    j. Financial
    k. Engineering
    l. Manufacturing
    m. Sales
    n. Service/Industry
    o. Computers
    p. Religious
    q. Entertainment, Media
    r. Journalist, Columnist, Author
    s. Other (please specify): _____

35. Are you a Homemaker? Yes No

36. What is your annual income?
    $6,000 to $18,000 $45,000 to $60,000
    $18,000 to $30,000   Over $60,000
    $30,000 to $45,000
    Are you annoyed at this question?   Yes   No

37. Do you have children: ages 1-10 11-18 19-24 24-up None

38. Are any of your children in college?   Yes   No

39. Do you pay tuition?   Yes   No

40. Do you pay everything else?   Yes   No

41. Do they demand the best of every-
    thing?   Yes   No

42. Do you insist they get the best of
    everything (that you did not have)?   Yes   No

43. Can you say no whenever you would
    like to?   Yes   No

Your Spending Habits:

44. Did your family give gifts at:
    a. Birthdays   Yes   No
    b. Christmas   Yes   No
    c. Every opportunity   Yes   No

45. Were they generous or parsimoni-   Yes   No
    ous?

46. Did you receive an allowance:
    Regularly   Sporadically   None

47. Did you have to work for it?   Yes   No

48. Did you steal money from parents or
    friends?   Yes   No

49. Did you ever petty shoplift?   Yes   No

50. Did you want to get away from
    home?   Yes   No
    a. At what age? _____
    b. Did you?   Yes   No
    c. How? _____

51. Did you hoard things?	Yes	No
52. Do you constantly give things away?	Yes	No

53. a. Do you subscribe to more than
     ten magazines?   Yes   No
   b. Do you read them all?   Yes   No

54. Do you give to charities?   Yes   No
   a. How many? _____
   b. Regularly? _____ How often? _____

55. Do you belong to a health club? Yes   No
   a. Do you participate?   Yes   No

56. Do you belong to any organization? Yes No

57. Do you take responsibilities in that
   organization?   Yes   No

58. Do you cook at home?   Yes   No

59. Do you prefer to eat out?   Yes   No
   a. How often? _____

60. Do you give gifts on all holidays,
   anniversaries, celebrations?   Yes   No

61. Do you give gifts to *all* your family? Yes No
   a. Friends?   Yes   No
   b. Acquaintances?   Yes   No

62. Do you send cards to everyone you know on:
   a. Valentine's Day?   Yes   No
   b. Easter?   Yes   No
   c. Mother's and Father's Day? Yes   No
   d. Grandparent's Day?   Yes   No
   e. Halloween?   Yes   No
   f. Thanksgiving?   Yes   No
   g. Christmas?   Yes   No
   h. New Year's?   Yes   No
   i. *Did I miss any?*   Yes   No

63. Do you spend more money than you
   have on gifts?   Yes   No

64. Do you select *carefully* for everyone? Yes No

65. Is your regular food shopping:		
a. Carefully planned?	Yes	No
b. Compulsive?	Yes	No
c. Erratic?	Yes	No
66. Do you leave your shopping list at home?	Yes	No
67. Do you "stock up" in your pantry?	Yes	No
68. Must you have a "spare" everything?	Yes	No
69. Do you buy bulk when there are just two of you?	Yes	No
70. Do you buy what's on sale whether you want it or not?	Yes	No
71. Do you use your coupons whether you want the product or not?	Yes	No
72. Do you ever buy generic products?	Yes	No
73. Do you hide them in your shopping cart?	Yes	No
74. Do you buy treats or gifts for others in your family even if your budget won't allow it?	Yes	No
75. Do you have a budget?	Yes	No
76. Are you laughing hysterically at the last question?	Yes	No
77. Do you shop when you are stressed?	Yes	No
78. Do you file the bills in the waste-paper basket?	Yes	No
79. Do you pay your bills immediately?	Yes	No
80. Do you borrow from Visa to pay MasterCard?	Yes	No
81. When you eat out, do you eat the most expensive dish on the menu:		
a. If you are paying?	Yes	No
b. If someone else is paying?	Yes	No

82. Do you eat the cheapest:
    a. If you are paying?   Yes   No
    b. If someone else is paying?   Yes   No

83. Do you believe that you have to pay
    later if you use your credit cards?   Yes   No

84. Do you shop from catalogs?   Yes   No

85. Do you look through the catalogs
    that come to your house?   Yes   No

86. If you can't sleep at night, what do
    you do to relax?
    a. Listen to music?
    b. Drink?
    c. Eat?
    d. Take medication?
    e. Call a friend?
    f. Call a 24-hour catalog service?
    g. Call a hotline?
    h. Get involved in some sexual activity?
    i. Write?
    j. Read?
    k. Other (please specify): _____

87. How often do you buy clothing?
    a. For a special occasion
    b. Seasonally
    c. All the sales
    d. Constantly
    e. Rarely

88. Do you constantly think of money?
    a. How to get it?   Yes   No
    b. How to spend it?   Yes   No

89. Do you read financial newspapers?   Yes   No

90. Do you read books on handicapping,
    blackjack, etc.?   Yes   No

91. Are you afraid there might be an
    unexpected bill?   Yes   No

92. Is every penny accounted for?   Yes   No

93. Do you debate with yourself regard-
    ing purchases?   Yes   No

Your Health:

94. Did/do you smoke:
    a. Occasionally?
    b. Frequently?
    c. All the time?

95. How did/do you get your cigarettes?
    Buy   Beg   Borrow

96. What kind of mood are you in by December 24th?
    _____

97. What kind of mood are you in by December 26th?
    _____

98. How does your stomach feel in January when the
    bills start coming in?
    a. Sinking
    b. Constricted
    c. Fluttering
    d. Not concerned

99. How is your blood pressure December 24th to 26th?
    a. High
    b. Low
    c. Explosive
    d. Normal

100. How do you treat people around you December
     24th to 26th?
     a. Dismissing
     b. Angrily
     c. Calmly
     d. Patiently
     e. Other (please specify): _____

101. Do you have regular physical check-
     ups?   Yes   No

102. Do you think physicals are a waste
of money (especially if the doctor
does not find anything wrong)?   Yes   No

103. Do you suffer from:
a. Migraines?   Yes   No
b. Intestinal problems?   Yes   No
c. Back pains?   Yes   No
d. Asthma?   Yes   No
e. Indigestion?   Yes   No

104. Do you read medical books?   Yes   No

105. Do you "catch" other people's
symptoms?   Yes   No

106. Do you take over-the-counter medi-
cations to deal with these discom-
forts?   Yes   No

Your Social Life

107. How do you spend your spare time? _____

_____

108. Do you watch television:
a. Sports?   Yes   No
b. "Wealthy Shows"
   Dallas?   Yes   No
   Dynasty?   Yes   No
   Rich And Famous?   Yes   No
   Soaps   Yes   No
   Others?   Yes   No
c. Shopping channels?   Yes   No

109. Was/is part of your recreation
"hanging out at the mall"?   Yes   No

110. Did/do you window-shop?   Yes   No

111. Was/is there gambling in your family?   Yes   No
a. Sports betting?   Yes   No
b. Regular card games?   Yes   No
c. Bingo?   Yes   No
d. Casino?   Yes   No

112. Did you take extra-curricular
     lessons as a child?   Yes   No
     a. Ballet/dance?   Yes   No
     b. Gymnastics/swimming?   Yes   No
     c. Crafts?   Yes   No
     d. Arts — music, drama, painting?   Yes   No
     e. Organized sports?   Yes   No

113. Did you stick to the activities in
     question 112?   Yes   No

114. How long? _____

115. Were you a member of a youth
     organization?   Yes   No

116. Do you have friends of your own
     sex?   Yes   No

117. Can you enjoy yourself without
     spending a lot of money?   Yes   No

118. How do you have fun? _____

119. Are you careful with money?   Yes   No

120. Could you be considered miserly?   Yes   No

121. Do you think that vacations and
     evenings out are a waste of money?   Yes   No

122. Do you have a physical reaction
     when you have to spend money?   Yes   No

123. Are you always "after a buck," even
     on social occasions?   Yes   No

124. Do you think in "cost"? For example,
     do you "price" what you see in
     people's homes?   Yes   No

125. Do you tell people how much you
     paid for your possessions?   Yes   No

126. Do you comparison shop for small
     items — *everywhere?*   Yes   No

127. Do you lend money to people and
constantly remind them of it?   Yes   No

128. Do you pass out when you get the
bill if you have invited someone out
to eat?   Yes   No

129. Are you being rigorously honest in
answering these questions?   Yes   No

130. How do you feel after all these questions?
    a. Relieved
    b. Happy
    c. Angry (please explain why in
       comments section below)
    d. Stressed out
    e. Confused
    f. Bitter
    g. Resigned
    h. Determined
    i. Reflective
    j. Promising you'll never agree to do
       another questionnaire

Please add appropriate comments: _____

_____

_____

If you have adult children, you might give a copy of this
questionnaire to them. Don't push it — try to be discreet.
We always seem to see what others need rather than
ourselves. Sharing our experience is wonderful. Unfortunately, we parents of adult children tend to be as delicate
as an atomic explosion when trying to "make *them* see"
whatever we feel in our infinite wisdom they need to see!
I believe we don't want our children to suffer as we did.
You know the answer to that one — all we can do is
inform and then quietly *pray a whole lot* without tearing of
hair and gnashing of teeth.

Survey Responses

I evaluated the responses of 157 people to the questionnaire for this book. The responses received were from:

Males age 35 or younger — 19
Women age 35 or younger — 30
Males age 36 or older — 22
Women age 36 or older — 86

One result of the survey that presented itself to me strongly was how many of these people were raised by two parents. I have had an ongoing battle for years with authorities who have blamed the plight of children on single parenting.

All those who responded to this questionnaire were adult children of dysfunction. Some of them were still very co-dependent. I had a biased group. None of these questionnaires were handed out to so-called "normal people" because that's not who this book refers to. This is credit, cash and co-dependency. Therefore, it was co-dependent people's opinion that I wanted.

Out of the 157 people, ten were raised by a single parent, four by grandparents and the rest by two parents. All but nine have siblings. Six had a parent in the military, 37 parents were professional and the rest were blue-collar workers or homemakers.

Out of the 157, only ten people knew the family income when they were growing up. One person knew it sometimes. The vast majority had no idea.

Another factor that was interesting to me was that most of the participants in this survey became professional people even though most of them came from blue-collar families.

The overspending/underspending in the family of origin was extremely dysfunctional. Several people were victims of ill health because parents refused to spend money on nutritious food or visits to the physician. Some of them have major problems with their teeth because they never went to a dentist.

About 60 percent received an allowance regularly and about 40 percent sporadically. Only 12 people out of all those who responded to the questionnaire wanted to stay at home. The rest wanted to leave, some from the age of four. The average age was 12 or 13. This research is not a professional project. For more specific research studies, please refer to the work of Dr. Robert Ackerman, one of the foremost researchers in this area. He is excellent at translating the scientific aspects into emotional behavioral situations with adult children. The reason I did this questionnaire was to get a general overview of the kind of problems that people grow up with. Therefore it is not a scientific review.

Reading through all the questionnaires, I used the metaphysical side of me to get a feeling of the despair and concern. One strong awareness I had was the level of denial. I would be reading some of these questionnaires and my gut would be saying, "No. This just isn't so." When I interviewed some of these people, it was evident that they could not be rigorously honest because of the message given to them early on: "What goes on in this family stays here." The level of loyalty was so strong the message was still there. Secrets and shame are always evident.

A vast number of the people who completed this questionnaire were very independent. Most of them paid for their own education. Practically all of them bought their own cars, with the exception — and this one surprised me too — of 20 whose spouses bought the car for them. Some of them, as I did from time to time, inherited the old car when the spouse bought the new car.

The vast majority were depressed when holiday bills started coming in. Some of them were relieved that the actual holiday was over, but the down side was very strong.

There were many complaints of poor physical health — migraine being one of the top in terms of suffering. It was with these answers that I had a little difficulty believing so many people raised in such severely dysfunctional families were totally without stress, but many replied they were *fine*. As you and I know, there is no such thing as a stress-free existence, so I got a little suspicious then.

There were a great many gamblers in the families of origin. In some cases it wasn't racetrack or casino betting, but wanting everything more. It meant taking risks to have a bigger house, bigger car, more successful business or more businesses — anything to look better. It seemed according to the interviews that these parents got on a roller coaster of believing that the more they had, the better off they were. This put them into a stage of denial when it came to looking at what they really had, which was "paper." They had a collection of loans and second mortgages to purchase what looked good. They were property rich and penny poor.

I remember during my first marriage when I lived in a huge house, we once had a garage sale. People came to the house, looked around at what we had out there and asked "Is this all? We expected this house to be filled with antiques." That home was filled with nothing, but the facade was good. That was my co-dependency: more secrets.

What was interesting was how many people were very reflective as a result of this questionnaire. When I talked to some of them later, they said they thought of things that really had never occurred to them before. One example was money being the basis of a lot of fighting in the family — spending it or not spending it. Another issue was favoritism as to which child got the money, gifts and clothes and how that came about, which was very traumatic in their memory.

A crucial part of the survey asked how they dealt with their situation today with regard to their own spending. Many of them spent compulsively. More of them spent erratically. One woman explained it to me, "If I don't do it all the time, then it's not a compulsion even though I seem to have an awful lot of things I don't need at the end of the month. I didn't do it constantly and compulsively. It was erratic. That was the difference."

Although the questionnaire was very important, it merely gave me an overview of the situations people had experienced in growing up. The real meat of the information was granted to me graciously by these people in interviews.

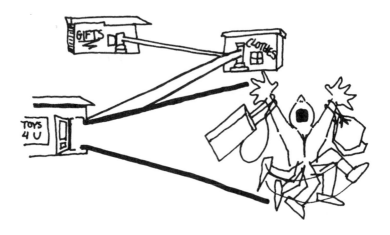

3

How Does Our Dysfunctional Childhood Affect Our Spending Habits Today?

I'd like to express my gratitude to everyone who completed the questionnaire and gave me permission to list just some of the remarks at the end of it. I think they are pertinent.

- I feel like you've stripped me and I'm standing naked with all these people. I'm anxious for you to fix me.

- I finally realize that my problem is due to money.

- Many of these answers would have been different in my first ten years of recovery. I feel

more focused and am gaining healthy money goals that
are realistic for retirement and supporting children. Unfortunately the first ten years had too many other issues
to explore.

• I really tried to be honest in my ACoA and incest
recovery. I find I am changing almost in terms of being. I
don't care about money.

• I am waking up to debts and lack of money in our
bank. My husband, also an ACoA, is very controlling about
money.

• My father died when I was 12, after a two-year illness, during which time we lost our house and business.

A whole lot of pain here.

• I am aware of patterns in the family and repeating in
me, but I am working on it. I also seem to go in spending
waves—books, clothes, fabrics. I look for value. If I feel I
can really afford something and I really want it, I buy it.

This one sounds like me:
• I love filling out questionnaires. It makes me look
honestly at myself. It was fun.

This middle-aged woman came up with something quite
interesting.

• My father bought me a coat when I broke my engagement. This is how I learned to deal with pain. I just
realized this recently. I'm being aware of the money problem and I'm trying to make changes.

Suzanne Somers, in her book *Keeping Secrets*, refers to
the method her mother employed after a night of drunken
terror with her father. "We didn't talk about it. We cleaned
up the mess and — went shopping." For a lot of years
Somers would buy herself out of pain, incurring major

spending problems. Her example is not unusual in dys-functional families.

> • Like you said, we do the opposite of how we were raised but I am feeling much better *now*. Seriously, it was an educational experience and quite revealing.

Incidentally, of course, these were adult children so there was a great deal of criticism: "The questions could have been better organized," "They weren't specific," "It was too long," "They were too specific," "It was too short," "There should have been 'sometimes,' 'possibly,' 'maybe.' " All I could think of was, "But you're trying to get well. So you write what you want to write. That's what the comment list was for."

After the holiday question, one woman said, "I used to be depressed in January and February. Now we have a combined income of $70,000. Five years ago I would have answered this questionnaire differently, but I am in recovery and live one day at a time. I used to get physically sick and feel guilty for weeks if I paid a lot for an outfit. Now I buy things only on sale and love it when I get a bargain. I'm getting better at buying things for myself. My boys even ask if I have a coupon for an item they want to buy." Lady, you're a success!

I was amused, yet sad, when I read one woman's questionnaire telling me that she suffered from migraines, intestinal problems, back pain and acne. Then she said her health was good and she wasn't stressed. I thought, "The denial is going to kill you if you don't do something about this pretty soon."

Here is something that sounds very familiar:

> • Money burns a hole in my pocket. I can't seem to control it. I tried to follow where it goes and it frustrates me. My mother always got a headache and got sick whenever she spent money. My husband saved and deprived me of the way I wanted to live, too. When I get money, I spend

it. I don't have a budget and don't know how to handle money. I don't understand it. I make a mess. I can't understand what happens and then I hate myself for being so stupid. So money works out to be a really painful relationship and I am scared. I worked full-time during the 17 years of my marriage but never saw how to use money to improve the quality of my life. I had hand-me-downs and a teddy bear. Now I have all kinds of stuffed toys, clothes and jewelry and many bills. Now because of people like you, I don't hate myself anymore and understand there is no way I could know how to deal with money since no one showed me anything. But I am willing to learn. I am going to Overspenders Anonymous after completing this questionnaire.

Thank you.

• I realize that I get high on bargains and want them all the time. I buy for others (bargains) but may keep them. Feel guilty about spending but love it.

How often have you bought something for someone, loved it and kept it? It's hard to let go of things, isn't it?

• This questionnaire has given me the opportunity to look at my spending patterns and how I've tried to buy friendships. That's a big part of compulsive spending. I have a new awareness. I do not connect money with fun, probably because money was the basis of constant traumas during my childhood.

These are all women so far, incidentally.

• My husband and I are financially harmonious. We balance one another. I'm the spender. He's the saver. Without him I would be in financial debt. Being in debt doesn't bother me at all.

• I have trouble spending money without feeling guilty. I must have 100 pairs of earrings and clothes I can't even find. My father was cheap. So men had to prove their love by buying me gifts. Of course, I have an understanding of this now but my money thing is still very uncomfortable. I don't want to deal with it at all, except of course to spend it. I'm not out of control, just uncomfortable, guilty. I feel like there's not enough. I can spend like my mother, feel just as guilty and then hoard it like my father.

• My father resented my mother's success and tried to control her by controlling the emphasis on money. To her other things were more important like character, being kind, respecting yourself.

• My wife and I earn about $130,000 a year. I owe an enormous amount of money to doctors, lawyers, credit cards. We have no savings. We live in a shack. Money's a major problem in our life. We make no effort to make a budget, a plan. Continue to live as if there was no tomorrow. At the same time we are totally committed to our children's health, happiness and education.

• I have been in recovery for over 20 years. My financial life has not changed one bit. It pisses me off.

• I started compulsively spending money as a teenager in response to my mother's alcohol abuse problem. I would buy clothes to make me feel better about her drinking. I'd charge them and tell her she told me I could buy them. 'Last night, don't you remember?' Of course she couldn't. Obviously, somewhere I buried why I was spending money until very recently.

• I always go shopping when I feel depressed. I get a high from all the beautiful clothes. Then I spend. Then I feel guilty. I promised myself I would pay my charge bill and not spend. Can't do it. One time I paid $68 on my charge and walked out having spent another $750 on a new charge. I was out of control. All of this precipitated by depression after an argument with my ex-husband.

This is like having a fight when you are an alcoholic and using it as an excuse to go out and get drunk.

• There was much shame in my family for being poor. Many people would blame my parents for having so many

kids. Today I will not ask for money. My husband and I
keep our finances separately—no joint anything.

These are just some of the remarks that were made.
The overall response was, "You're ahead of your time
with this one, Yvonne." That didn't surprise me. This is, I
suppose, the last bastion to be scaled. The amount of
protection around oneself, in terms of money, can only be
compared to the depth of shame involved by having it and
not having it.

To attain a happy medium in terms of finances, a great
deal of introspection is necessary. Like other shame-based
problems, the family of origin and its messages are major
issues. So many people have told me that their sense of
worth is tied up with the amount of money involved in
their upbringing. In addition, money has been a major
pressure in many people's lives in terms of accomplishment. There is a great deal of guilt attached to money
being spent to "improve" a child and the child not wanting
the improvement.

Co-dependency And The Money Connection

One of the tragedies of our time is the overwhelming
preponderance of young people who commit suicide. One
of the considered causes, among many others, is that parents—in their zeal for their children to have and do better
— plan for that child's life while it is still in the womb.
Many times people raise their children to believe they are
going to be doctors, lawyers or whatever. The child's capabilities or desires are not even considered.

A lot of people share the tremendous amount of guilt
they feel when they have not fulfilled their parents' desires and justified the amount of money spent. In their
later years adult children often feel a responsibility to
care for their parents because of what they have been
told they owe. That's not good parenting. Good parenting
is to do for your children what you want to do . . . without any thought of return. Guilt, money and shame go

hand in hand, as these questionnaires have proved. This is confirmed by the discussions held when I teach a one-day seminar on this subject.

Although the questionnaire does not play a major role in this book, it has given some information and indicated that even though I am "ahead of my time," it is good to begin at the beginning. What is most important in my mind is that I can only take people as far as I have gone myself. This kind of investigation and writing only fuels my own personal desire to continue to grow and deal with the substance called money.

I Shop. Therefore I Am.

Chapter 4

Do You Have
A Problem
With Money
Or Is Denial A
River In Egypt?

Denial is a big part of money issues. Recognizing that fact is essential in any addiction. As the whole business/professional/social world is a giant selling machine, it is difficult to see over- or under-spending as a problem. Television commercials scream at us that in order to live a better life, we need more! more! more! There was never a better description of this insanity than the book *Blind Faith* by Joe McGinniss. Joe has a natural genius as a writer. As a social commentator he has no equal:

So normal had shopping as a form of recreation come to seem that when the newspapers wrote their summer holiday roundup stories: "The beaches were crowded; boat traffic on the bay was lighter than expected; state parks reported heavy turnout," they would include the activity at the major shopping centers: "The Ocean County Mall was filled to capacity this holiday weekend as avid buyers with no better way to occupy their spare time once again made thousands of unnecessary purchases." . . . You were what you drove, you were what you wore, you were where you lived, no matter how heavily mortgaged it was.

It's the old keeping up with the Joneses. "Anything you can do, I can do better." The competitive edge — but for what? To fill up that empty, yawning void of personal insufficiency.

I suppose the major question is: Do you have a problem with money? To find out for yourself, take a look at the Assessment List and complete the answers.

Do You Have A Problem With Money?

Assessment List

	Yes	No
1. Do you have a deficit of money at the end of each month?	___	___
2. Do you save carefully and then binge spend?	___	___
3. Do you buy in bulk when you do not need to?	___	___
4. Do you use coupons whether you want the food or not?	___	___
5. Do you buy "friends" in your life who are emotionally unavailable to you?	___	___
6. Do you file your bills in the wastebasket?	___	___
7. Do you use credit cards and react with surprise when the bill comes in?	___	___
8. Do you buy gifts or give money when you cannot afford it?	___	___
9. Do you suffer with migraine headaches, intestinal problems or back pain?	___	___
10. Do you have anxiety attacks around April 15th?	___	___
11. Do you spend to keep a relationship going?	___	___
12. Do you sweat when you have to spend money on necessities?	___	___

Denial

When I first started writing this book, I had no idea how enormous and diverse the problem was. Considering that denial is a great part of any addiction or dependency, recognition is the first step. With a whole business/professional/social world dedicated to the "money" attitude, it is difficult to see over- and under-spending as the severe problem that it is.

Co-dependents are extremists. They rarely do things by halves, and that includes finances. Whether the person is a spender or a miser, excuses run in abundance.

Denial is a major issue. In order to recognize that there is a problem, these people have to reach their own bottom. They, too, have their enablers and their rescuers because money is an important part of self-esteem. Imagine anyone in *our family* having to go to court, declare bankruptcy or be sued for nonpayment. We can help them just this once. Anyway, they promise it will never happen again. That's like giving a junkie the rent money to keep him out of your neighborhood. It just doesn't work.

The misuse of money has a direct connection with childhood experiences. Money, whatever way it is accumulated and utilized, can be another anesthetic.

Children learn the value of money very young. They see it used as a weapon to control, to tempt, to create guilt, to reward, to manipulate—and children learn well and fast from their role models. They are exposed to parents with money troubles, and they see the change of mood and behavior when the check arrives. They watch what is done with the money in hand—do the parents forget the famine now that they have the feast? Or do they prepare intelligently for the next time? How long does peace reign? Do children calculate how far they can push until they get what they want, like Mom or Dad did? Do they listen to the lies?

"I just don't know where it all goes!"
"I keep within the budget—I can't seem to get ahead!"
"I ask you—do you see me in the shopping malls?"

It isn't surprising that many people are cross-addicted in the areas of food and money. The excuses, denials and resistances are very similar.

"I can't seem to lose weight and I never eat a full meal!"

Like the non-meal eater who lives on constant snacking, the non-shopper makes hay with the catalogs that appear on a regular basis in the mailbox or the good old "shop-by-television" channels that know how to handle boredom.

This is a great sociological problem—*boredom*, ennui, call it what you will. People addicted to auctions, bingo and casinos are all fighting boredom. Add to that the get-rich-quick syndrome and the problem grows. Pathological flea marketers and garage sale fanatics are all looking for a bargain. What about bulk buyers? Same problem—they've found a gem! The hoarders never let go of anything—"just in case!" Ask them, "In case of what?" *No answer.*

"But I Never Go Shopping!"

A few years ago I was up to my neck in denial. I was in extreme debt and couldn't understand why. I hated malls, couldn't abide shopping, moaned and groaned when bills came in and the money wasn't there.

"Where does it all go?" I would wail. "I never go shopping. In fact, if I go to a store with a friend, within minutes I want to leave."

Whenever I used to get upset and couldn't sleep, I wouldn't think of picking up a drink or a drug. I would do one of two things:

1. Raid the refrigerator and cupboards and eat continuously anything that didn't move.
2. Pick up a 24-hour catalog and call them with anything up to a $1,000 order.

Then, after the fix, I fell asleep. I could still say, "I don't like to shop," with pride lifting me above my sister shoppers. "The woman is such a perfect professional. She doesn't need to stoop to shopping."

When the order showed up, I would panic and tell my son I had no idea where it all came from. I would examine every item and return it by UPS.

My favorite catalog is Spiegel. I actually coined a new verb—to *spiegel*: I *spiegel*, you *spiegel*, they *spiegel*.

Where Does It Come From?

Pathological spenders come in two varieties: those who spend on themselves and those who spend on others. Who is the sucker group? No contest—they are equal. Both of these addicted groups are covering up a great deal of inadequacy, whether real or imagined. The spending is the excitement, the drug of choice. One person may buy 12 identical dresses of different colors—with accessories and jewelry to match—for herself. Another may be incapable of buying anything for herself but spends inordinate amounts of money on children, spouses or friends. The pathology is the same. The anesthetic for pain is the goal.

Where does it come from?

Like any other compulsive behavior problem, money dysfunction starts because messages from early childhood, verbal or non-verbal, took root. What are some of them? The following were collected from my own childhood and from participants in workshops on the subject of money:

1. Money never bought happiness.
2. It is better to give than to receive.
3. As long as you are happy at what you are doing, the money isn't important.
4. The love of money is the root of all evil.
5. Diamonds are a girl's best friend.
6. Money makes money.
7. Money can buy anything and anyone.
8. Rich people save their pennies.
9. Nice people don't talk about money.
10. A penny saved is a penny earned.

11. Waste not, want not. (How many of you were told about people starving in India if you didn't clean your plate?)
12. Receiving a bill in the mail means they don't like you.
13. It's just as easy to fall in love with a rich man as a poor man.
14. The less money you cost me, the more I like you.
15. It doesn't matter what I do, I can't get ahead (handed down from generation to generation).
16. I'm property rich and penny poor.

What were your messages? Make your own list now.

How about buying gifts for people, even some you don't know very well? For example, you go to the wedding of a friend's sister and take an expensive gift. Why do you buy gifts when you can't afford to?

1. Because they'll like me more.
2. I'll feel accepted.
3. It's a wedding! (Very indignant!)
4. I'm an impulsive buyer. If I see it and like it, I'll buy it, rather than shop for something more affordable.
5. It's expected. (By whom?)
6. I don't like looking cheap. (Yvonne says: "Doesn't bother me anymore! What a trip!")
7. I don't do it often but when I do, I overspend. (Classic analogy — "I only drink on weekends!")
8. I like to see people smile and be pleased.
9. Guilt. Sometimes if I have given something nice, I feel bad if I don't give someone else the same. If you've given something once, you have to give something better.

This last one is usually associated with relationship insecurity and jealousy, whether with a lover, a parent or a friend.

Hoarding

Compulsive spending is something people have suffered from unknowingly. It is an addiction that rarely gets much attention because few recognize the many facets of the problem and the addict may be highly deceptive. There is much denial involved with money and spending issues. Money issues include not just spending it, but hoarding it.

People who are hoarders can be in severe danger. Not only can it be a health hazard to collect things in terms of space, for example, but imagine the bacteria these things can collect when the house is jammed. Hoarders come up with all kinds of excuses—"I might need it one day." (Like a miser, this is where it is dangerous. A miser would say, "I bought a new suit 25 years ago, why would I want another one?")

An extreme example I heard of was a reclusive woman whose family was worried because she refused to eat. She said she wouldn't spend money on such waste. "Waste?" they said. "What do you mean?"

Her amazing response was, "If you buy food, you eat it. It comes out the other end anyway. What a waste." She finally starved to death. It wasn't anorexia, as a lot of people wanted to believe; it was simply that she would not spend the money. Even if her family took food to her home, she absolutely refused to eat it.

The pathology with hoarders is that they cannot give things away. Neither can they sell them. They simply cannot. It's no good saying, "Look, why don't you get someone in who can sort out all that stuff?"

They say, "No. No. I can't."

"But you haven't opened that box for 25 years."

"I know, but there might be something in there I need."

"Well, let's look now."

"No. I don't have the time now."

"You don't do anything else. When will there be time?"

Like the alcoholic who wants to get to the bar but doesn't know how to get out of the house, the hoarder will start a fight or retreat into silence—and leave the scene. The people left behind know they don't dare remove one particle of dust, even if they feel it would resolve matters. Hoarders guard their possessions because they make them feel safe. Some hoarders were born into extreme poverty and only "things" give them the security they want.

Paper Hoarders

Then there's the newspaper/magazine/periodical/article collector!

"I've got to read that article . . . one day."

"You never know. I might need this for a research project."

Sometimes when a patient is blocking or as part of one of my women's groups, I'll get them to do a collage. I ask them to bring in three or four magazines they are willing to cut up, glue and scissors. (Of course, my own bias is that they are not allowed to mutilate *National Geographic!* I don't know what there is about that magazine, but they have to stay whole.)

I ask my clients to go through the magazines, cut out anything they relate to and glue it onto a large white sheet of paper from a flip chart. Then, depending on the positioning of the words, pictures and statements, we can interpret the collages and break through some blocks. The preparation for "Operation Collage" should take approximately 45 minutes. After one-and-a-half hours of warnings from their fearless leader — me — magazine hoarders are still reading articles they never had time for. At each exhortation from me, they add to their "I'll read it later" pile. The collage takes forever! The remarks are hilarious and the behavior impossible. Fortunately, they can laugh at themselves when they realize what they are doing.

Jeremy's Story

Not so with Jeremy.

Jeremy was a paper hoarder — anything readable.

His wife Maggie would cry and tell me she couldn't get into the living room because of all the reading material which Jeremy never looked at after he got it home.

"Come on, Maggie, you're exaggerating. You must be able to get into your house."

Next week Maggie brought me photographs of the house. Not only was the living room jammed, but so were the entrance hall, the bedrooms, the den and even the bathroom in case he wanted to read while using the facilities. Of course, he was more likely to read the labels on the back of the cleaning agents or deodorants. They really couldn't move in the entire house.

Now I know this next piece is hard to believe. But stay with me.

Jeremy, who was of relatively comfortable means, *purchased the house next door!* His refusal to get help has gained him another house, which is rapidly filling up, and has lost him his marriage. He is a "little upset" about it but has chosen his disorder because, as he says, "You can't trust people to be there but you can trust things!"

Maggie is doing very well, thank you.

Hoarding comes in various degrees. When I first moved out with my two sons, I had large boxes of "things" cluttering up a room I wanted to make into my little sitting room. I procrastinated (sound familiar?), always bemoaning the fact that I had nowhere I could settle my work or myself with some privacy. My son Daniel would offer to help me sort through this stuff. I always refused, saying I had to do it myself.

One rainy day he walked into my bedroom with a large box of trash bags and said, "Mum, let's do it." I started to protest that I might need "those things." He said, "They've been there for over seven years. What could you possibly want?" And out it all went.

If you are having heart palpitations, anxiety attacks or the cold sweats reading that last paragraph, you've got the problem! It was very freeing for me, but scary too. What I learned was that I was not a compulsive hoarder but a symptomatic "past collector." When that went, so did a lot of the pain. You might not have the pathology of hoarding . . . only the difficulty of letting go of the past. Get someone to help you organize. There are those who do that professionally.

The extremists of this condition not only hoard, but will not spend either. They are holding on to past history and letting go of nothing. This is a very serious problem. There is a difference between intelligent saving, or even disorganized clutter, and hoarding. People die from that latter kind of behavior. They won't seek medical help if they are ill, won't buy seasonal clothing to deal with the climate, won't get any help that is needed. Howard Hughes is probably the most famous example of a person who hoarded, became a recluse and died in pathological solitude in spite of his wealth.

Some people fear going to doctors partly because they are afraid of what they might say. These are the ones who state, "Well, you had it your way. I went and had a damn physical and the doctor couldn't find anything wrong. I spent $85 and—nothing wrong." What a state of mind! Instead of gratitude that it only took $85 to be pronounced healthy, they saw it as an infringement of their rights. Most of the fear is around the fact that it costs something.

This is an exceptionally difficult condition from the treatment angle. As with most compulsions, self-esteem and the erasing of childhood tapes seem to be the leading problem. There is simply no recognition that hoarding is unhealthy.

The Dangerous Extremes

It may seem that what I am saying here is it's a question of "damned if you do and damned if you don't" and as a parent you must be always on guard and very careful what you say. That is not so. Actions speak much louder than words, as we all know. If too much attention is put on material things and not enough on the person — their behavior, their feelings, their thoughts — then what we produce is a generation of insecure people. In order to set the matter straight, I am fully in favor of people having pretty things in their lives—a nice car, a lovely house, a good job, good clothes to wear and interesting things to do. I consider all that to be normal.

Hoarders, overspenders and underspenders are extremists. It is the denial element within that extremism that causes the difficulty. For people to have to buy a certain number of things in order to stop feeling any discomfort is a serious psychological and emotional condition.

What kind of pain is hidden by these bizarre behavior patterns? The most important one has to be feelings of low self-worth. I may believe if I hold on to things, they'll never let me down. Of course, I can't trust people like that because *they* have a choice. But inanimate objects and possessions do not have a choice. They have to stay with me until I choose to give them away — should that day ever come.

Just recently I read an article about a well-known and wealthy sports person who took a trip into a very bad neighborhood where the people were so grateful that he stopped by. Then he spoke out about situations that were not to his liking. With all his millions, it never occurred to him that he might want to give some of it away. I found out later, talking to him, that he's too afraid to give anything away because of his childhood poverty. Somebody needed to tell him that you don't go to poor neighborhoods and leave nothing behind other than the memory of your brief visit.

I often wondered why I hated window shopping. I never really knew why and on reflection I see that as part of my denial. To me, window shopping was an exquisite form of torture, like the carrot dangling before the donkey's nose, always just out of reach. Window shopping, to me, was looking at things I could not possess because I had no money. True, there were small things I used to shoplift. But I couldn't afford the things I really wanted to make me feel feminine. Looking at windows full of these things only made me more aware of the painful absences I had in my life.

I have to watch that assertiveness at all times now. I know how different it is for me. Although I don't like shopping, if I need to buy something, I will go and buy that one item. I will not go from store to store looking at what is there. I still have that from my childhood. Maybe one day that pattern will be broken, as we will all have to break many, many patterns regarding our spending, saving and holding on.

Can you recall some of the habits with which you grew up? Hoarding, collecting, saving? And why? Having experienced wartime when everything was scarce, we always bought as much as we could when it was available. Our pantry was jammed to capacity. Ask your families—if they are able to share—what it was like if they were in:

1. The Depression
2. The Holocaust
3. Any kind of military conflict

Ask what their possessions represented to them. If this is not possible, remember "shopping" and "groceries" especially when you were a child. I believe you'll be surprised at your recall. Please write about it and compare it to your attitudes and behaviors today.

The Hoarder, The Underspender, The Collector.

Chapter | **5**

The Cost Of
Living And —
Sometimes —
Dying

Money is a mysterious product. It gives pleasure and it takes it away. Why do people have so much trouble with or without it? Because it buys people, things and even places, which most of humanity believe bring happiness.

This is not so. To have money and earn money is acceptable, even desirable. To have it for the power it brings and the belief that life will then be beautiful is the same as having cosmetic surgery without altering the inside.

People abuse money. They either have no respect for it or they hoard it. Either way it brings discomfort and despair.

A healthy attitude is to keep money in its proper perspective — to be used to survive and provide the basics of living, to bring pleasure, to understand its value, to be controlled and not controlled by.

In our culture so much is gauged by what people have, not what they are. If there is an inadequacy, real or imagined, in a person, money might well provide the anesthetic. More dangerous are the people who use money to fill in the gap — but who have no money of their own. Then the creation of dysfunction occurs. Like the dieter who constantly thinks of everything connected with food — measuring, calculating, weighing — so is the problem spender absorbed with money. Do I have enough? Do I have to spend it? Will a gift make amends? Will he choose me over her if I spend more?

So it goes. The endless unanswerable questions denote the problems that need to be faced, not suppressed by money. The level of denial is deep and corrosive.

Obese people are frequently heard to wail, "I can't understand this weight gain. I never eat a full meal!" No, the constant nibbling takes care of that. So it is with the spender. "I don't know where the money goes . . . a quarter here, a dollar there . . . it just disappears." It's no surprise that food and money addicts are sometimes cross-addicted in these two areas.

People who are addicted to money and possessions usually have severely damaged egoes. Possessions give them identity. As co-dependents have no recognizable identity, the money issue is a big one.

If I Spend Enough, They'll Love Me

Imagine chasing the impossible dream of having the perfect family. Having experienced many relationships with emotionally unavailable people, the co-dependent subscribes to an ever-growing myth that there will be some kind of gratitude if material things are provided. What these people end up with in their relationships is a bottomless pit.

Janie's Story

Janie was one such woman. She fell in love frequently and immediately took hostage. Like most people who want to rescue, she kept finding the perfect victim. Usually he was attractive, slender with soulful eyes. It started like this: "I had a terrible childhood, Janie."

Then would come the litany of the ills that had befallen him, this poor but handsome man. Jim would end his sad tale of woe with, "But I deserved being beaten — I must have. After all, my father was really a good person."

How noble. He's getting through to her. But she still has her smarts — until . . . good sex! "Honey, you're the best between the sheets." Janie has never had a satisfactory sexual relationship, so *this is love!* Eventually Jim doesn't feel like working because no job recognizes his talents or pays him enough, and anyway, he's too sensitive to drive, so how would he get there? But Janie is there to help. She comes through with the rent, the food, the chauffeuring, the entertainment and whatever else this darling boy deserves.

This wouldn't be quite so bad if only Janie had the money to do it. Janie wouldn't dream of taking a loan out for something for herself, but she has no qualms looking into the possibilities for Jim. She over-extends herself to please and to be accepted. That's a credit, cash and co-dependent problem right there.

Where did she learn this? Many people in the relative insecurity of their childhood would "buy" friends. Countless people have reported they would steal from their parents to buy gifts for their "friends." Janie used to take money from her father's wallet when he was drunk. She was shy and fearful, but other kids thought her snobbish. So when any kind of party came around, she was overlooked. Her "generosity" opened the doors, but it was surface acceptance. When the money ran out, so did Janie's "friends." The habit remained until all of Janie's relationships took on the same pattern. She couldn't say no and was too afraid to present herself empty-handed. So when a hint would be dropped about what Jim needed, what he wanted and how happy it would make him, that was all she needed to hear.

Janie's life was empty. Like many people in her position, she believed the treatment meted out to her was what she deserved. She knew no better, having been raised in a family where her mother constantly appeased her father with his addiction to beautiful things, women and luxury. That was Janie's frame of reference. She couldn't understand why she never felt safe, loved or appreciated. She would analyze the situation, never coming up with any resolution. She only knew one way to behave — give and keep on giving.

Co-dependents give or spend until it hurts. Who's hurt? Think of our language.

"I bent over backwards for him." How very painful, to bend over backwards. Maybe it's okay for a contortionist.

"I went out of my way to buy her the ring she wanted." What for? People "go out of their way" because pain is the way, and the pain has to be circumvented *at any cost.* (See the language? "At any cost." You can always tell a recovering spender!) So people "go out of their way" to do for others, to buy for others. Then more is bought to ease the guilt of spending. It's a vicious cycle.

Let's look at how co-dependents circumvent pain. What do they do to make themselves feel better? This is the root of all addictions and the core issue that needs to be dealt with to stem the addiction. Overeaters state that when they were growing up, the reward was food.

"Let's go and get something to eat" — social life.

"If you are very good, I'll get you some ice cream" — conditional love.

With spenders the rewards are material. I have said it myself. "If you feel lousy, go buy yourself something."

I Shop — Therefore I Am

Freda's Story

Freda was a spender. Bright, warm, intelligent and as pathologically co-dependent as they come, she was a brilliant and well-known actress. Her problem was massive — no privacy.

When depressed, Freda would *need* to buy a dress. Off she would go to the mall, her favorite hunting ground and return with not one, but 12 dresses all the same in different colors. She couldn't buy one pair of shoes; she had to buy 12 to match the dresses. Then came jewelry, scarves, makeup — the works. As can be imagined, this woman always looked like a million dollars. *(There I go again!)*

But Freda was all surface. I have since met several male and female Fredas whose lifestyles are identical. They are addicted to 12 — each sign of the zodiac.

She was in terrible pain from a severely dysfunctional family, being the only child of parents who lived solely for one another. She had been married five times. She was emotionally distant from her four children. No one knew of her pain.

I remember asking Freda about other relationships. She would never invite anyone to her home. She trusted no one and it took a very long time for her to trust me. When she did, a most amazing tale unfolded.

Her finances were totally out of control. Her spending had taken her into unmanageability. She admitted the primary motive for decking herself with adornments was to win her parents' love and acceptance. They were very external people. She would threaten to visit and, even though she was world famous, they would make excuses. She would become hysterical and they would come through — that time. The cycle continued until one day Freda decided to take a risk and tell me a secret.

The answer to my question, "Why don't you have friends? Why don't you have people over for coffee?" brought these answers:

1. The house was filthy, even with a cleaning lady.
2. A great deal of the shopping she did was a "fix" only. Many of the packages remained unopened — all over the house.

3. She was afraid of people knowing her personally. Although she was a public figure, that was surface only.
4. She would laugh a great deal when things hurt her so people were never secure with who she was.
5. Being a well-known actress, her face was instantly recognizable. She constantly had the fear that she would be found out.
6. She would try to hide her poor hygiene habits by smothering herself in expensive perfume.

When I first started working with Freda, she was suicidal. She told me, "It doesn't matter what I do to improve myself, nobody seems to want to be near me off the set. I don't even know what my problems are, other than the fact that when I earn a lot, I have no money. I have all these things cluttering up my home. I don't know where to start first."

She would not, up to that point, confront her underlying problems. It was just too painful. Each time she felt the pain, she would go and spend more money. We had to define the basis of the problem.

What was the major issue? She had not been wanted. She was a nuisance. She was a dolly to be dressed up to personify the beauty her parents deified above all else. Tragic. This is Rokelle Lerner's "frosting on the rotten cake" syndrome, Ann Smith's "looking-good family."

Not only had Freda always been a "performer" for her parents and friends growing up, she became an ornament to her various husbands. She was beautiful, accomplished, and a victim of the assumption that beautiful women are happy and have good lives. Her problem was that she would succumb to being that ornament. A man would say, "I feel so proud to have you on my arm," and that's what did it.

Although her depression was severe, she had a great deal of difficulty in connecting this situation with her family of origin. These people would spend any money in the world for everyone to look good. They were co-dependent/emotional spenders.

I had great difficulty in trying to break through that intense ivy-covered barrier that was almost choking Freda to death. Until she was prepared to look at what was happening within her emotions, her addiction would continue. She would spend more and more to fulfill that addiction. She refused to look at the withdrawal factors — how painful being empty was and how positive and conducive to her recovery it would be to stay in that empty feeling for a while.

She called one day to tell me she had left her fifth husband and was living in a car. She had finally realized she just had nothing and she felt there was no reality to her existence. After a ten-minute call, I convinced her to come and see me again before she made any further decisions.

At that point, having divested herself of any claim to fame she may have had, she turned herself entirely over to me to do with whatever I would. The first thing I did was put her into a 28-day treatment program for co-dependency.

She did very well. Her denial about spending, they told me, was incredible. After the third week they began to chip through very slowly. A lot of push/pull double messages were given to her growing up: "Come here, I love you. Go away, I can't stand you. You're my darling girl, but the Van Browns are visiting so stay in your room. You'll never be as good an actress as your mother, you know. It doesn't matter how hard you try."

Not only did she have problems from being this dressed-up little dolly and being an ornament, but she also heard that she could never even think of achieving her parents' status. The pain of recognizing those messages hit her hard. The therapists were able to help her start reversing the decisions she had made and start learning the difference between decorating to hide oneself and healthy intelligent dressing. What they did was sow the seed.

When Freda came back to me, she was euphoric. She was ecstatic. I told her about the book and she said, "You

have got to write about me and give them my name so
they know for sure this is a reality and they can check it
out. Maybe we'll even do a movie about it — you can write
it and I'll act it."

I had to point out that went against my belief system.
She was too early in recovery to break her own anonymity
and deal with the astronomical amount of shame surrounding money issues among adult children from dysfunctional families. It was difficult for me to do this without her feeling put down or let down. I explained to her,
as anyone would explain to a newly recovering addict, that
when you start that addictive behavior, your emotional
development shuts down so you are still very young. She
and I had to work together on her slow recovery. She
needed to look at me not as her mother, but rather as a
supportive person to whom she could talk when she
slipped without being afraid.

Freda has great determination and she used it in her
recovery. She got rid of all her credit cards. She found
herself a business manager. She got a new agent to replace one who had been robbing her. She went regularly
to meetings for adult children of dysfunction and overspenders. She is doing very well now.

The Money Trap

Many health professionals treat symptoms in this money problem area, but the root of the problem has to be
addressed. People with compulsive spending habits do not
buy because they like to buy. It is the only way they can
feel good. It is their fix.

They are considered to be irresponsible. It is not irre-
sponsibility. I won't go so far as to say it is a disease, but
I do know it is a severe and painful condition. It is an
uncontrollable dependency that engenders the same kind
of self-loathing as other severe and obsessive behaviors.

When people are doing, doing, doing and giving, giving,
giving until it hurts, they get hurt. We give until it hurts,
as Janie did, and nothing happens. This is called emotional

spending. Nothing changes, although that is what we really want: to change people. Compulsive spenders, givers and doers are into the "if onlies." "If only I do this, maybe they'll treat me the way I want to be treated."

I seem to get a great deal of information from unlikely sources. As a devout and dedicated mystery book aficionado, I am constantly reminded that the connection between money and violence is strong. Frances Fayfield, in her book *Not That Kind Of Place,* describes life in a comfortable London suburb:

> He reflected that this brave new world was trapped economically in marriage, like a welfare couple in a slum, neither with another place to go and no money to split up. The only difference was that one couple was more affluent and lived in a different cage where the padding didn't really help. There were plenty of murders in these situations, plenty of scope for them in cozy Branston. The upwardly mobile, striving for heaven, by some accident untrailing their choices rather than expanding them, were leaving themselves no time to think. No time to see how the children thought either. Would they prefer the posh schools or the concrete playgrounds? Electronic toys or cardboard boxes? There was no time to judge your partners here.

So many people are trapped in their lifestyle. Money is an enormous part of being trapped. It creates illusions of well-being, or lack of it, so people stay stuck. It manifests itself in rationalizations. "If I leave, how will I survive? How can I change my way of living? I'll never make it. What about the children?"

Surprisingly, children adjust much quicker than adults. My children, for example, adjusted to living in the United States much quicker than I did. I experienced much pseudo-guilt about uprooting them from friends and family, when in fact it was my own grief I was avoiding.

So it is regarding money and unacceptable relationships. How many young people remain at home because it is less expensive to do so? This situation is perfectly all right, if the conditions emotionally and personally foster contentment. If the relationships in that household are intolerable and people still stay, it is usually because they do not want to lessen their mode of living. It seems sensible to me that if you aren't happy where you are, you get out, even if you have to take a room somewhere without all the physical comforts of home. Of course, it is much more difficult with children involved, but it can be done.

I stayed in my marriage for 24 years before I decided, sink or swim, that was it. Why did I wait 24 years? Well, I learned a lot of things through my own recovery and working with people. One specific is: Women don't think they can make it financially on their own, even though most of them can. That's been drummed into them since childhood. We come from a socio-economic, Judeo-Christian background that tells us women have to be dependent and we are just not going to make it on our own — no matter who or what we are. *That's not true.*

I have believed for years that my Higher Power will come in and present something to push me to make a move. As with the most trusted professionals in my life, people who use humor to deal with me are most effective. So it is with my Higher Power. Like many other people I would say to myself, "Why are you here? Why are you putting up with all this stuff? Just because you are living in a huge house with a big car, you don't have to stay living like this." You can manage, even though it might be tough. You can still manage.

The strongest message was: "You've been married for 24 years. You know what's going to happen at 25? You're going to have this big silver wedding party thrown for you by your children. All these people are going to come with lovely gifts of silver and say to you, 'Isn't it wonderful? Twenty-five years — congratulations!'" I started to laugh and said to myself, "No damn way!" It was that piece that got me moving out of the situation.

I then found the strength and courage to know I could make it and that I did not have to perpetuate my own dependency problem by living with someone who insisted on living well beyond our means. I was born into that, raised on it and married into it. But I created my own dysfunctional spending patterns *for which I am responsible.* When my husband and I were dating, I remember that he would spend about three times his salary on a gift for a friend. I should have seen it then but "should have" doesn't prove a thing. I knew that I wouldn't ever live beyond my means again. I spent the next ten years doing just that because it was a frame of reference in which I had been raised and I was accustomed to it.

So there I was looking at this silver wedding anniversary and deciding no. I wanted no more of it. Even with my education, my self-esteem was pretty low. Certainly I wasn't working anywhere remotely close to my potential. I had no money, no job and two dependent children. And I said, "I don't want to be married anymore." Just like that.

This is sound advice: *Don't do it like that!* Planning is necessary. Save a little. Take some courses. Get a reasonably paying job. Arrange child care. Do it all before you go. You won't get any help once you leave. *Don't do it the way I did it.*

There is rarely a reason for people to stay in their own pain emotionally. Changes do not take place because people create reasons from their past experience to keep the status quo. It is familiar. The pain of its discomfort is like an old friend. And what do we say? "I just can't afford to do anything about it!" Well, maybe at first you can't. If you continue to say it, you never will. That repetition is simply another way of not moving.

The Courage To Change

Michael's Story

Michael wanted to tell me his story for only one reason — to that date, no one had believed him.

In his youth he was a self-described kleptomaniac. What he did was shoplift to give gifts to his mother in the hope she would stop hurting him. His father had left her and the family.

When he was old enough to sustain an erection, Michael became his mother's lover. He was 11. His mother was into whips, chains and pain — some sadism, more masochism. She would hurt Michael sometimes. She demanded that he beat her, tie her up and make her bleed. Are you horrified? Not Michael. This was his normal.

His mother not only demanded sex from Michael, she wanted to be courted with presents and flowers. Where was an 11-year-old to get such things? Theft. Over the following six years Michael became very adept at obtaining gifts for his mother. It never occurred to him that this kind of lifestyle was abnormal. He simply lived the Jekyll and Hyde existence between home and school. His school activities were severely curtailed as Mother wanted him home at nights to be her companion. Friendships were discouraged — and girls? Forget it!

At age 16, Michael was arrested for shoplifting. Apparently he had been watched for months and there was no way out. He was put on probation since it was his first arrest. His probation officer felt there was something radically wrong, that this was not a simple shoplifting gig. All the articles were feminine and Michael was masculine in his tastes. As the story unfolded the probation officer was astonished, not at the level of incest, but at the matter-of-fact telling of it.

Michael was removed from his home to a group home for boys. Unfortunately, that was the extent of it. He received no treatment.

I'm wondering about the impression you have so far of the socio-economic status of Michael's mother. She was a highly paid, assertive, aggressive business executive in a large, prestigious company. When this event occurred, she was about to be named vice president of this company. While Michael was in the group home, she committed suicide.

Michael eventually left the group home and attended college. He began to date and suffered great difficulty sexually. Remember his introduction to sex. He became what he describes as asexual because the guilt and confusion were so overwhelming.

He wanted me to write about his unconscionable situation and record that he felt blessed to recognize that he needed help. His spending was outrageous. He said, "I couldn't perform sexually without pain being involved, and how could I tell the women in my life of such dark shame? So I bought gifts, more and more and more."

Michael had an exceptionally lucrative position and could afford expensive gifts. He spent as he earned and had nothing in reserve. It was nothing for him to give a woman a diamond necklace on a first date. As the gift-giving became more and more expensive, Michael sought help.

He found an excellent sex therapist who helped him resolve his agonizing issues of guilt over the incest and his mother's suicide. As he worked with his self-esteem, the spending resolved itself. He now has a wonderful wife who is more interested in his loving tenderness than intercourse and who patiently awaits his continuing journey on the path to recovery.

Regardless of one's past history, if recovery is desired and joy demanded from within, it can and does happen. Bravo, Michael!

How is it, then, that Michael did so well? It sounds as if his life is perfect now in spite of his deeply-damaging childhood trauma. That depends on your definition of perfect. It suits Michael. He has created his own new norm because he had the courage to pursue counseling and to realize his own goals. He attended a lot of seminars, such as those by Brian Tracey, Fred Pryor and Dennis Waitley. He read books by Og Mandino, Elisabeth Kubler-Ross, Viktor Frankl and others. He found help in the many articles I have written on the subject of self-esteem.

He told me once that he read an article in which I said, "Each person has the right to a respectable self-esteem." He had no idea what I meant. He mulled it over in his mind before finally picking up the phone and asking me about it.

I explained to Michael that because people don't know how to focus on themselves, they don't know what they require in order to feel healthy. Respectable self-esteem is that happy glow one gets being comfortable in one's body and within one's own soul. It harbors no feelings of guilt, shame, envy, jealousy or possessiveness. He said, "How do you do that?"

I said, "You know what? I'm on the journey right now. Why don't you come with me?" I shared with him the things I had to do to relinquish those feelings and fears that kept me in my marriage, in my sickness, in my feelings of low self-esteem and no self-worth. Matters were further complicated for me by the incredible financial problems caused by constantly buying people. I needed to learn balance and that's what I shared with Michael. Just going into therapy to see me and to see the sex therapist wasn't enough. That was good but it wasn't enough. That was simply what gave him the key to unlock the door to his emotional fortress.

He also had a brain and potential he didn't know how to use. He is an exceptionally bright man, aged 29 now. I said, "You've got to get into this motivational training. These workshops are excellent for you."

What Michael did was one of the first things people have to do: made a commitment to himself to do whatever it takes.

Motivational seminars can help you do that. One has to be selective, but most programs are not terribly expensive and a volume of education is available. There are many, many tapes you can listen to and I recommend that you do. They can help you touch that call that goes beyond the brain, into the gut, into the subconscious mind where it all happens.

You see, the major problem is that scarred individuals, such as Michael, the walking wounded, have no idea how to deal with the pain and agony of their confusion. When Michael was taught that he was not responsible for his mother's behavior, the sickness of her sado-masochism, his father's absence or his mother's suicide, he had to put the focus on himself.

To tell someone who is really wounded to do that is like telling a little child it is time to go to the supermarket and prepare the meals for the week. The most predominant problem in all of this is his *feelings* — "It was all my fault. Therefore, I don't have the right to feel happy and content. I don't have the right to have money and good things. I know deep down nobody is going to love or like me just for myself. So I have to spend. I have to buy. I have to give. I have to . . . "

Again, let me restate: "You can change no one but yourself."

The focus is always on the other person in unhealthy environments. We co-dependent persons must understand we cannot change anyone other than ourselves. If our significant others don't want to change, they will not. People who compulsively overspend need desperately to be accepted. They must learn to accept others as they are, without attempting to create guilt or obligation by spending money on gifts. It is a hollow, empty, non-rewarding behavior.

And Now A Word From Our Sponsor

I refer once more to the book by Joe McGinniss, *Blind Faith*. This is the true account of the murder of Maria Marshall of Toms River, New Jersey, allegedly by her husband, Robert Marshall. It is a gruesome tale of money, sex and greed. It is narcissism to the maximum: murder.

A native of Toms River states,

> Actually, except that Rob Marshall happened to be there with his wife's dead body, and he could hardly claim that he had never seen her before, he is only functioning exactly the way TV commercials tell him to behave. Get it. Get it now. Get it at any cost and then get another one.

Even death is apparently a small price to pay for having one's needs met.

The last excerpt from Joe McGinnis's extraordinary book brings us to the effect of advertising when it comes to spending. The pressure of the media is beyond belief. Have you ever noticed, especially around the end of September or October, the number of toy commercials that come on? Usually there is a message about how desperately important it is for your child to own this particular battery-run something or other. Messages urge, "Be the first kid in your class," or "Be the first child on your block" to have this, to wear this, to possess this. Again, emotional spending.

Watch The Commercials

I'm asking each of you to take a look at how much television commercials affect you. Take one evening, sit in front of the television for three or four hours and pay special attention to the commercials. They do two things: They take away the reality of life and they also create a method of thinking to make you believe you will be a better person by owning that product.

What do I mean by "take away the reality of life"? Television commercials are strategically placed. Suppose you are watching a film and it is really intense about drug addiction or rape or something else that is very traumatic. Right at that precise intense moment when you are beginning to really feel what's going on, the commercial will intervene. And it is usually something lighthearted to take your mind off the trauma. So we're not allowed to really feel. If you don't believe me, watch and see how strategically commercials are placed.

The other aspect addresses the quality of your life. If you don't have whatever the product is, then you can't possibly be living up to your potential. As I'm writing this book the wars between Coca-Cola and Pepsi Cola, AT&T and Sprint, would be absolutely hilarious were it not for the fact that millions of dollars are involved which could be better spent. Pay special attention to commercials. These are created by bright Madison Avenue psychologically-oriented people who know exactly what they do.

I believe that we can learn a lot. I realize that if I dislike a commercial intensely, I can't really remember the product unless it is one I particularly like and I think the ad producers fouled up. For example, a Mueslix ad features a man who talks about the cereal in some kind of pseudo-foreign accent and terribly overdramatically. It really did put me off Mueslix for a while. If ads make me laugh, I usually do remember the product. There are some commercials that are just fun. Now thanks to my Higher Power that I am healthy, I can look at these and laugh. I don't have to run out and buy everything. I remember somebody who did — my mother. I always knew which program she was watching by what was in her cupboard. She would buy and try everything.

Have you thought about the danger of headache commercials? We are never, ever taught to go to the source of the pain but rather to deaden it. Isn't that what this is all about? Denial. The denial of pain — physical, mental, spiritual and emotional.

What do people say when you are in that pain? "Go out and have a good time." Even a company featuring motivational materials sent me a series of cards. One of them was: "Celebrate when you have completed your job. Go out and buy yourself something." There's nothing wrong with that if you are not a compulsive spender. However, there are other ways of rewarding yourself without spending, spending, spending.

When you do your list of commercials, please do it under three headings: ones that make you laugh, ones that make you sad and ones that make you angry. I think you will be surprised at your list. Take the time to do it one evening and be aware of your feelings when you watch these commercials. I guarantee you will go through the gamut of feelings during those three or four hours.

I Need It!

Chapter 6

The Rich And
The Afflicted

Money, especially inherited wealth, is no protection from co-dependency or addiction. Like other co-dependent people, the wealthy are often unaware of their own identity. In many cases the bonding relationship for a child in a wealthy family is with a servant, a nanny, a cook. Children frequently have to live with a parent who married into the money and simply does not know how to behave or what is required.

The frame of reference is fuzzy at best. Direction often comes from the hired help, who can be fired on a drunken whim, hardly a secure situation.

Children of wealthy dysfunctional parents are paren-
tally starved and victims of benign neglect. It is benign
only because it is in a mansion, not a slum. They are
raised in splendid isolation. They know nothing personal
about the servants who raise them and have no feelings
for the absentee parents who are going about their hectic
social and business responsibilities. The confusion is un-
bearable. These children don't know who they are, they
have the best that money can buy but can relate to no one.
They are empty, afraid and unaware of feelings. They
sense obsequiousness in the company of "lesser mortals"
because money is power. It earns respect. People are careful how they handle rich people. There is an air of mystery surrounding them that precludes any intimacy or
even approach. They are envied, yet they are lonely and
frequently look with longing on the rich family lives of
those with less money, power and control.

The expectations of the wealthy child are often unrealistic.

Morgan's Story

Morgan is the only child of wealthy divorced parents.
She ran away to get married when she was just 16. Her
parents gave her a huge house for a wedding present. She
had no idea how to organize, manage or control a paper
bag, much less a house. She was in such fear and no one
would help.

"How lucky you are to have such a beautiful home," her
envious friends would say. Morgan came into treatment
with me on her 40th birthday as her fourth marriage was
ending. Morgan had led a life of chronic depression, anxiety, low self-esteem and unworthiness. She was beset by
guilt for being one of the "haves" and not one of the "have
nots." When we met, she could not string a sentence together. She is a talented writer but could not write a
word. Frustrated beyond belief, Morgan had tried everything short of giving her money away.

So she decided to do just that. She decided the money was so alienating that it had to go. Luckily, we caught her in time to make some recommendations to safeguard her future years. But the rest went. What a metamorphosis! She laughed, exercised, ate right, got a job and put herself through treatment.

The rich and afflicted do not have to be that extreme. They do, however, require intensive therapy, as often their sheer frustration at trying to experience some excitement leads them to socially and legally unacceptable behavior.

Categorically, I can say to you now, never envy the wealthy. They look as though they are having a good time because of the money involved. However, those who are children of dysfunctional parents suffer no less than any of us, maybe even a little more. They face a great many problems:

1. The social and business lives of their parents. These children are usually raised by the servants.
2. They get bored very quickly. Nothing excites them. They can replace any object or possession as fast as it is broken. They never have the joy of saving up for something.
3. They trust no one outside of their financial equals. How do they know when people like them just for who they are, not what they've got?
4. They have been everywhere, seen everything and met everyone, all at a very early age.
5. Even though they crave excitement, they don't know how to get it. So they frequently become alcohol and cocaine addicts or get involved in some life-threatening "hobby."

Along with money goes power. Imagine a bunch of adult children/co-dependents/addicts with all that money and power. It's like being in a fairground with all the funny mirrors, noise, confusion and running, running,

running — looking for some sanity. They are all seeking to live as children with adult financial responsibilities. They have no frame of reference for what is normal and no social skills to deal with anyone out of their own class. So what does this produce? Rebels or very, very good children.

Even the Bible lambasts the rich. Blessed are the poor and the meek, we are told; and it is easier for a camel to pass through the eye of a needle than a rich man to enter heaven. And of course there is, "The love of money is the root of all evil."

Children of emotionally detached rich and afflicted families suffer more with secrets. The families are terrified of news hounds, knowing that the populace loves to see the mighty fall. With that in mind, money and what it can provide offer the only solace.

Mike's Story

Mike had inherited money from his father, not a huge fortune, but enough to live well without having to work. His father inherited it from his father. There was a lot of shame around it. His grandfather had tied up the money very tightly so it paid out the interest but the capital could not be touched. Mike's father hated this whole set-up because there was never a way he could get into the money to get a business started and do well on his own. The extraordinary thing was that Mike's father, even though he hated the control, did exactly the same thing. Mike refers to this as "control from the grave."

Mike was 12 when his grandfather died. The message from him was, "You will never have to worry about your retirement." That's one hell of a message when you are 12 years old. As a consequence, he really developed no interests.

Mike said one of the things he inherited from his father was a lot of shame for not working for a living. His father was an alcoholic and had extremely low self-esteem through not working. He was very rigid in his thinking and class conscious, with an English orientation. He was emotionally and physically unavailable. Mike's mother's family had had money but it was lost in the Depression. Her siblings were alcoholic.

When you consider that Mike was raised by two people who both had low self-esteem, carried a lot of shame and were caught up in the world of alcoholism, he really didn't have much frame of reference on how to behave socially, in school or anywhere else.

He told me, "From the time I was about five until I was in my mid-teens, my father was at home — his lawn mower business was there on the farm and later he was retired. But emotionally, of course, he wasn't there."

Mike was dyslexic. Not only was he abused by other students at school, he was abused by the teachers and they encouraged his fellow students to abuse him. In fact one of the things Mike said which was absolutely mind-boggling was, "I felt that Dickens was normal."

If you recall some of the novels written by Charles Dickens, such as *David Copperfield* and *Great Expectations*, they demonstrated the cruelty that children experienced, especially poor children in the 1800s. Here was this wealthy young man in the 20th century considering that kind of experience normal. What incredible pain!

Mike went to a boys' school and had a rotten experience. His teachers considered him stupid because of his dyslexia. He had absolutely no one to turn to. Finally the school sent him to a psychologist who tested him. The test results revealed that Mike had an IQ of approximately 130!

You think that was good news? Instead, it was another dilemma. Before testing he was stupid. After testing he was lazy. The personal shame was unbelievable.

What did Mike do to survive? In his head, he completely isolated. His behavior became more erratic and he began to act out but still isolated. He said when he went to school, he would steal comics from the stores. He stole a lot; I imagine because of the addiction to excitement that he experienced. He also learned to self-nurture with things and money which led to later problems with money and work.

When Mike wasn't in school, he was working back on the family farm. Some of the chores were expected but for work beyond those chores, he was paid the same as other farm hands. It was an 80-acre farm and he really worked hard. He had a younger brother and sister but was very lonely.

He said, "My brother and sister were close to me in age, but we were never close emotionally. I think I was unable to form close bonds from early childhood." He would build special places for himself where he could live in his own fantasy world. He used barns and haylofts to create special places. That was his escape.

Mike was alone in the middle of the nuclear family. He didn't really belong with his parents and he didn't really belong with his siblings. There was a complete emotional void. In fact, he couldn't remember any good relationships, including his experiences in school where he tended to be a victim and was beaten up. What he can see now was that the whole relationship between his grandfather and his father was dysfunctional because of the control of the money. He inherited that dysfunction along with the income.

The message that came to Mike very clearly from his grandfather and father was that he was not capable of handling his own affairs. He felt robbed of any self-esteem and ability to make decisions because the capital was so tightly tied up that he couldn't use it to get ahead in business.

"My father never got far in business. I, on the other hand, was very successful in one business. However, I burned out after two or three years of 60- to 80-hour weeks."

When I write about Mike or his father I'm writing about almost the same kind of treatment they both received from their parents. Mike's father worked with his grandfather, and that was another deprivation because he was not allowed to pursue his chosen career and be an engineer. Grandfather, who held the purse strings, said no.

Suddenly one day, grandfather fired father. Just fired him! Mike sees this as his grandfather stripping his father of self-confidence and then just telling him to get out and make his own way. He started a lawn mower business and did very well, but there was always that feeling of extreme tension — remember, everything was very rigid. Mike said he could remember at age 12 going to Christmas dinner and having to wear a dinner jacket. Everything was proper but the pain and frustration was evident. He remembered it from his father and obviously his father remembered it from *his* father.

Mike's father was a very disturbed person. He was unhappy and frustrated, never having realized his ambition of being involved in engineering. He was very good at what he did, but still was completely controlled by money. Those of you who don't experience this could say reasonably well, "Why didn't he just get away? Why did he have to rely on the money? Why didn't he just go to work? He started his own business. He must have done well. Why was it that important?"

Stripping someone of their self-esteem and self-confidence doesn't happen overnight. When you are told you will not have to ever worry about money, when you are put on a fixed income that never changes with the economy and when you are raised from childhood with that kind of attitude, it is very difficult to break away emotionally and psychologically. There's a whole lot of shame around this.

This slow realization Mike had that "everyone's father works but mine," was the same realization that his father had about his own father. Yet his grandfather did work. Both Mike and his father were emotional prisoners of this man. His father ended up selling a lot of their silver gifts from the wedding to raise capital. Then when he started his own business, he enjoyed it. But eventually he became just like his father — very dominant, alcoholic and controlling. And he set up exactly the same trust fund that his father had done. His safety factor was to be very controlling.

Finally Mike's father committed suicide. He just couldn't take the emotional isolation anymore. Again if you have

not experienced this kind of controlling atmosphere in your
early growth years, you may have difficulty comprehend-
ing this emotional imprisonment. But if you have been in
other kinds of disastrous relationships where you have
stayed and gone back for more and more and more, you
realize this is not just the money. Maybe you can understand it on that level when you ask yourself, "Why do I
keep going back?"

As Mike mentioned, he never had any good relationships. He did get married once for about two and a half
months. The woman had married him just for his money.
She left in a hurry when she found out the money was all
tied up and Mike could not get his hands on it. He still
can't. He's made his own way and developed his own life.

Kitty's Story

Mike's current wife, Kitty, was an only child raised in a
blue-collar neighborhood. She was raised by two incredible snobs with a low income. The best way she describes
it is, "My parents wanted to be Mike's parents. They wanted social acceptance. They wanted the self-esteem, the
money, the acceptance." They didn't have any of it. It was
a totally different culture in and out of the house.

Kitty's family would fight constantly about money. Nothing was new — used car, used rugs, used furniture. They
fought terribly. They would talk about being in the poor-
house. She was afraid to go home from school — afraid
all their belongings would be on the sidewalk and the
house up for sale. Her father also was an alcoholic, very
rigid and similar to Mike's father. There were a lot of
rules. He was domineering and was a Jekyll and Hyde just
enough to keep her off balance.

Her mother apparently was a very earthy person, set in
her ways. Her father was rigid and unyielding.

Their community included Italian and Irish children
who went to Catholic parochial school and a few others
who went to public school. Kitty wanted to go to public
school but had to go to a Lutheran parochial school be-

cause her parents thought she would have a better education. For some reason they managed to find the money for school even though they couldn't find money for anything else.

In addition to this, Kitty was also part of a triangle as the only child. Her mother was the earthy person but an incredible snob and wanted "only the best for her." Her father took her to bars and made sure she kept the secret. They were a secretive family. When Kitty was in third grade her mother went to work but kept it secret from her father for over a year. What they presented outside the house in no way was typical of what went on inside the house, where there was perfectionism and martyrdom. Kitty's mother was a perfectionist and a martyr. She smoked a lot, worked a lot, ate a lot.

Kitty was very bright and daydreamed a lot. She was never allowed to do anything. Her nickname at home was "Stupid." She was abused emotionally and physically. The family actually was ultimately shunned by the church because the mother had a fight with the preacher. Kitty did, however, have a lot of friends in the neighborhood, so she was able to separate the physical and spiritual poverty within the home from her behavior outside the home.

Kitty's early life was incredibly restricted. One of the joys of her life was that she was very athletic, but her parents were so afraid she would become lesbian as a result that they restricted her. They always said, "Act like a lady," "Don't carry on," "Be quiet." She was as much in an emotional prison without money as Mike was with money.

When she first met Mike, she was totally overawed by him. She didn't really care whether she had a relationship or not. Apparently Mike, who is a big man, had a reputation of being mean. There was also this myth about him that he was incredibly wealthy.

Maybe the next generation of this family will be, but Mike has to live on his income. It's sufficient for him not to have to work but it isn't enough for him to be able to do anything specific. Bear that in mind as you are reading this. It's like being retired on a fixed income.

Mike was into drugs at that time whereas most of Kitty's boyfriends had been alcoholics or certainly drunks. Mike apparently had a good time with drugs. He enjoyed himself. Kitty had been married once before, was the breadwinner in that marriage and had always worked. She had known what hunger was with no one to turn to. Then all of a sudden here was this possibility.

Finally they got together, lived together for a while and then married. One of the things her upbringing had done was to make her believe she "should" have as much to contribute financially as he did. The attitude learned from her parents toward Mike was that she had to have money to equal his. She shouldn't be a "moocher." (Both parents were dead before Kitty and Mike got together.)

She discovered several years ago that she was an artist and a good one. Prior to that she always had guilt about not working. She did well in school but never really had any motivation or enjoyment. She never finished her graduate degree. So this sudden realization that she was an extremely creative, talented woman was incredibly exciting to her. It was almost as if all her years of poverty and her parents trying to groom her into something that would attract money didn't matter anymore.

Kitty and Mike are both in recovery from alcohol and drug addiction. They have worked hard at their marriage and are continuing to do so. She says he was difficult at first to live with because of his mistrust of women and his disastrous first marriage. She added her own set of problems to that. She still sees money as independence and in her life there is a tremendous emphasis on money — his. She's also honest enough to declare that she loves not having a job because that releases her creativity. On the other hand she'd like to make more money and feels she would like to contribute at times, which she does in terms of some volunteer work — as does Mike.

She loves not having a job and Mike loves not having a job, but at times they feel guilty about being unemployed.

So it's damned if you do and damned if you don't. The beauty of both these people is that they are working hard, individually, to deal with their pasts. They spend time together, but they have common interests and separate interests. Mike does some volunteer work in the area of alcoholism. They would both like to make more money and break the tie that has crippled them in terms of the way this whole thing was set up.

They are truly beautiful people.

"Doesn't Anyone Like Me Just For Myself?"

With all the money the "have nots" so envy, there is often no peace, no happiness, no contentment, no ambition in their lives. When there is an enormous amount of meaningless money, it is frightening to realize that is all there is.

Francesca Kness, a New York psychologist, grew up in wealth that she chose to hide from her friends. Working with the children of the wealthy today, she quotes from one of them:

> Everybody thought that because my family had money, they got me into schools, jobs, clubs. It was terribly demoralizing and by my early twenties, I felt totally unemployable.

With no self-esteem and no goals, these people feel they can accomplish nothing.

If a person has no ambition, feels no excitement, looks forward to nothing — money and possessions are empty. I am sure you have asked yourself on occasion why the children of the rich and afflicted get into trouble with the law. Why do they file suit against one another to get even more than they already have? It made no sense to me until I started treating the co-dependent and adult child community. The pursuit of excitement is the culprit here. When you are of average income, fulfilling an accomplishment after saving up either time or money is a thrill. Waiting for that special trip to the theater, buying that

slightly better automobile, going overseas for a vacation
for the first time. Can you remember those anticipatory
chills? Children of wealth rarely experience those.

I recall working with a patient who had just returned
from a ski trip. I asked him if he had a good time. "Okay,"
he replied.

"I've never skied," I said. "It must be so exciting whoosh-
ing down that slope."

He looked at me with great sympathy in his eyes.
"What's so great about it? I started skiing in Switzerland
when I was five — you ski down the mountain, then you
go up it again, ski down, then go up."

I felt a deep sadness coming from this young man, who
I believe wanted to feel what I knew I would feel if I could
ski. (As I write this I am sitting in Abington Physical
Therapy, Abington, Pennsylvania, with my right leg in a
whirlpool. I slipped and broke my leg on two feet of mud
in a nature center three months ago. Ski? I think not!)

Having no positive identity is not the prerogative of the
poor or the average-income person. These children of
wealth have learned to buy love and then to rarely trust it.

Barbara Hutton's Story

I recently watched a television mini-series about the
Woolworth heiress, Barbara Hutton. What a tragic figure.
I had grown up reading about the antics of Barbara Hutton
in which it appeared that she had a continuous round of
pleasure, fun and high jinks. I'd also read the other side of
what I felt to be an incredibly lonely woman.

When Barbara was four, her mother committed suicide.
Her father was an alcoholic and a womanizer and really
didn't want to have children at all. He left Barbara to live
with her grandfather, with whom she was very close.
Then when he died, she lived with her aunt and governess.

She had absolutely no frame of reference and with all
that money was totally helpless and a complete victim.
She went where she was sent. She had absolutely no say
about who she spent her time with. She didn't go to ordi-

nary schools, daycare or anything of that nature to meet with others to learn social skills. She was an isolated lonely little girl. Children were sometimes brought in to play with her and she gave them whatever they wanted. In one poignant scene in this mini-series three children came and she just didn't know how to behave so she showed them everything she had. Of course, the children felt she was showing off. She wasn't doing that. She just didn't know what else to do. When they admired anything, she said, "You can have it." One of the children wanted a music box that was her mother's, but she just couldn't part with that and said, "You can take whatever else you want but not that." This little girl picked out some classy toy, a doll of some kind. As soon as all three of them got what they wanted, they left. Then she just cried, broke all the toys, said she didn't want anything and wanted to give everything away.

I think one of the basic tenets many independently wealthy people hold dear is that money is their protection. The true position underneath is, "I'd really like to give everything away to see if people really like me for me." That's always there.

The trust level is very low and they always seem to have to stay with others of their own financial status. Barbara's father said, within her hearing at one time, that he never wanted to have a daughter anyway. He got himself another wife. The little girl was just pushed from pillar to post.

Her only real friend was her cousin Jim, who was in much the same position she was. He also became an alcoholic. He was homosexual. Whatever his behavior, no one could say anything because of all the money involved. As Barbara traveled all over the world, the British press called her a reject and a spoiled brat. She really was not a spoiled brat. She was a very lost child. No one, except Jim, ever really knew her. Her money position stood in her way.

Ironically, even her money kept her out of certain social circumstances. Because the money came from the retail business, she was frequently referred to as the "shop girl."

High society wanted her money because there were many of the impoverished landed gentry around who had a title to sell. They wouldn't give her respect, however. They just thought of her as *nouveau riche.*

So here she was, having been taught nothing except that if you want someone, you buy them. She was exposed to both men and women who would hang on just to be around her and get to be known as part of the inner circle.

She fell into the hands of her first husband, who was supposedly a Georgian prince. He and his sister planned the marriage for money, knowing Barbara would do anything to be loved. That's what she was trying to buy. Prior to the marriage, with the support of his sister, he and Barbara signed an agreement for an allowance for him. He constantly humiliated her. He even cheated on her on their honeymoon.

The first night of their honeymoon when he turned to hold her, he said, "Barbara," and you could see her anticipatory look. "Barbara," he said, "you're too fat." I can remember hearing those words in the mini-series and reading those words when I read about her and feeling the terrible pain. She wasn't fat at all and from that moment on ate very little. She was always painfully thin and very frightened to put on any kind of weight.

This man's spending became reckless and he humiliated her at every turn. She kept going back to him. He wanted her to divorce him so he would get money but she was just addicted to that situation, as co-dependents with money are. The more times she returned to him, the more money she spent. Finally, they were divorced.

Her second husband was supposedly a Danish count who did seem to have means of his own. He was like a Rasputin or a Svengali. He took over her mind and persuaded her to surrender her citizenship. He was a complete narcissist and I think probably a sado-masochist. He raped her. They had a child and he stole the child. Then she was accused of being a Nazi sympathizer because she was trying to help someone she cared about who was in the hands of the Nazis.

She finally got rid of her second husband. Not only did she want to buy love, but she bought freedom. So her money was spent on men in one way or another.

She finally got her friend away from the Nazis by paying someone off. They married. When she came back from a shopping spree one day, she found him in bed with another man. The fact was that she had absolutely no way of judging human beings.

As you are reading this, are you still envious of people who inherit wealth? It's very difficult for those of us who never had it to believe money can create such havoc and such pain. We all think we could handle it if we suddenly had wealth. I say, we have to get ourselves together first. There are countless people who can't cope with money. In fact, I was on television in New York with one young man who won the million-dollar lottery three times and had nothing left.

I found it fascinating that the only man Barbara Hutton ever married who loved her for herself was Cary Grant. She couldn't handle that because he couldn't be bought. His work and his schedule were important to him. She wanted him with her all the time and he wanted to consider his career. Her money couldn't buy that. So she divorced him.

There was one other man, very young, who had the same feeling about her. She had reached the point when she simply could not trust anybody at all, and even her money didn't work for her. When she finally died, this woman who had started out with her inheritance of $78 million ended up with approximately $3,000 in her checking account. It is a sad, sad commentary.

Money certainly demands respect in the Western culture (and probably everywhere else, but I am only aware of the culture in which I live). I observe very disagreeable people being treated with respect simply because they have money. There is a lot of power attached to it. I am grateful that I now have the spirit of the Higher Power deeply within me and am only impressed with real people.

Who Should Hold The Purse Strings?

There are some people, of course, who handle wealth
very well. They are in the minority. Please keep in mind
that this book is about money and *dysfunctional* people,
including those from rich families.

In one of the affluent areas in which I worked, group
therapy was conducted for those — especially men —
marrying into money. It is a very difficult transition.

In this area of cash and co-dependency, who is at fault?
Again, so much of this money was a direct result of "in
the name of love" attitudes. Ancestors who worked and
amassed great fortunes often came from difficult circumstances. They didn't want their heirs to suffer the way
they had.

Even in lesser affluence, we see parents working to
provide for their children above and beyond their needs.
As these circumstances appear, it is totally evident that
parents need some hard-core reality training.

Parents from any stratum of society who overprotect
their children are robbing them. "No pain, no gain." Life
is painful at times and if children have been denied survival skills, what will happen when Mummy and Daddy
are no longer around? There is a need for practical therapeutic application for the rich and dysfunctional who
hold the purse strings and decide how the money will be
apportioned.

Many wealthy families do not talk about money. Frequently it is in the control of a trust fund, which is sensible when enormous amounts are involved. However,
there are two aspects of trusteeship that need attention:

1. Are the trustees tough enough to withstand the requests of the heirs? Are they co-dependent, too?
2. How much money is available on an annual basis?

The first factor is important because these "children
of" have difficulty understanding *no*. As they mature, in
order to find that elusive excitement, their "wants" accel-

erate. "More! More! More!" is the cry. When parents are considering how to secure their estates for their heirs, it is essential to select people or an institution who know how to evaluate a request.

"Sorry you banged up your Porsche but you can't have another one. Get it repaired," is an example.

With the second aspect in mind, a realistic budget can be created with the help of an astute businessperson. This budget can provide for schooling, shelter, clothing, food and vacations — comfortably but not in excess. Certainly there must be some flexibility, especially as heirs prove they are capable of handling their own finances.

Usually children have important questions about family wealth, as they do about sex or grief. There is enough shame in dysfunctional families without further conspiracies of silence. If parents feel unable to relay this information, which is often the case, the alternative is to retain a professional who can. Parents would like things to be a little easier for their children than it was for them. Money can be an asset if used correctly.

If it sounds as though I am into punitive action for these young people — quite the contrary. I feel there is a terribly inequitable distribution of money in this world. If these people get healthy, they can help a lot of others who are in need. God knows there are enough of those around.

It is also a learning experience for wealthy families to cease bailing out their young. The co-dependency runs riot at times of conflict. If the self-destructive behavior continues, responsible treatment is vital. This often requires the services of an interventionist. It is unhealthy to use money as a means of control. However, if people are hurting themselves with it, money has to be withheld if the person is unwilling to go for help. Challenges and hard knocks do not render these people helpless.

The children of the rich and dysfunctional, like people with any kind of power, are tricky. They believe and they have seen that money and power can cure anything and everything. Wrong! Dysfunction is dysfunction, money or no money.

John Levy of Inherited Wealth Consultants of San Francisco completed a five-year study of the rich in 1986. Based on interviews with the wealthy and their therapists, *Coping with International Wealth* offers suggestions and counseling.

The Dependence Of Independent Wealth

On one occasion I went to a patient's country home for a few days. It was to be an intensive therapeutic workout as the blocks were becoming impassable. We drove up to her gorgeous house, she called and made reservations for dinner at the best restaurant, she hustled me into the car to look around the place and we ended up in a series of artisans' shops in the local village.

She picked up two pairs of magnificent hand-crafted earrings to buy for me. I protested that I was here to work and gifts were inappropriate.

"Poof," she said. And handed the salesperson her credit card. It bounced! They would not clear the credit card because the last month's bill of $3,500 had not been paid. She said, "I've got millions in the bank and I can't use a credit card. Obviously, the office didn't pay on time!"

I didn't know it, but she rarely handled money. Whatever she wanted — from a camera to a house — the "office" was simply billed for it. Only the Royal Family does that where I come from. I was relieved that I did not have to continue the discussion about the earrings, until she whipped out six more cards. At the same time she called the office and burned their ears off! After I calmed her down, she said, "Do you have any idea how hard it is for me to get a credit card or any credit for that matter?" No, I didn't know.

"Just think of all the questions on the application form: income, place of work, salary, established credit. I have none of the above and companies have to see evidence of financial responsibility. I don't have that. The office has had to apply for my card, so absolutely nothing is in my name."

I had not realized that the independently wealthy are so dependent. What freedom it is to earn your own money and spend it as you will, without having to gain someone's permission. No wonder there is such rebellion among the wealthy. She was mortified.

I thought maybe we could now get down to work. Not so. She simply could not relax — she had to entertain me. I told her I was being well paid for my time and I'd like to earn the fee. It was useless. She was on her own territory and she had to prove to me how worthwhile she thought our relationship was. When I finally got her to talk about the issues that had to be addressed, it was almost time to leave.

Finally, we talked about her behavior and her fears of intimacy. She admitted she simply didn't know how to behave any other way. She was so afraid that if she didn't give, entertain, fix, I would leave and not want to work with her ever again. At last I got her to see that she was a lovely young woman who didn't have to do that "buying" thing any more. She had to learn to trust her own judgment and to face the pain of people who left because they couldn't get what they wanted from her. The dependency on her advisors, trustees and guardians was enough to put up with. We decided to work hard on self-esteem and self-trust.

She then took me home. I felt we had accomplished something. She knew she no longer had to prove herself by providing for others. She assured me that she had heard me and would set about making her changes. I breathed a sigh of relief. As I unpacked, there was a magnificent pair of silver earrings in my suitcase. Oh well, back to the drawing board.

From Distorted Pride To Genuine Self-Worth

It's amazing what distorted pride can do, even if one is not in the category of "wealthy." From my childhood, I had always been with people who lived beyond their means. "If you didn't have it, lie about it." It was a no-no in my marriage even to intimate that we couldn't afford something. We couldn't "afford" a cleaning lady or a gardener, but we lived in a 20-room house with six bathrooms, two kitchens, three acres of ground, a tennis court and a swimming pool. I loathed the house from the start. It was a beautiful property if you could afford to live there reasonably — *with help.* We couldn't.

After seven years I finally moved to a little Cape Cod house very happily with my two sons. Daniel, then hosting a teen call-in radio show, once invited a young listener to come visit. Now, people have ideas on how "celebrities" live. Today I can say, "That's up to them to think what they please." This was five years ago. What did I whisper in Daniel's ear? "Why don't you take her to see where we used to live?"

Thank God, he looked at me in amazement and said, "We live here now — that was then." Out of the mouths of babes!

How much we create our own realities in order to be accepted. Instead of being proud and happy that as a single parent I had accomplished a difficult move, I sought to fulfill the expectations of this young girl (and I didn't even know whether she had any!).

Lessons Learned

What have I learned in working with the rich and afflicted? A few of the lessons are:

1. I've learned not to make judgments about other people's lifestyles on the basis of what "eyes see."
2. I've learned to count my own blessings.
3. I've learned that money can create as much of an emotional prison as poverty.
4. I've learned that the bottom line is self-esteem, self-worth, self-respect and self-confidence. That's what we all need to learn regardless of status and income.

If you are independently wealthy and feel stuck, please seek help from someone who really understands what this wealthy emotional prison is all about. Go to 12-Step meetings. If you are lonely, isolated and feel people don't really know and love you for you, then get involved in a 12-Step program and learn how worthwhile you are. It is difficult, but all growth is — until you reach that magnificent realization that you are worth it and you have the right to happiness. You have the right to enjoy what is yours — and that includes your money.

Buying Love

Chapter | 7

Enabled Or Enabler?

It was a mystery how my daughter's money needs always came up just at the time when I had a little money in the bank. Of course, it would not have mattered whether I had money for myself, I would have found it somehow for someone else. I always rescued, saved and protected. When I was a child, I was so invisible and demoralized in my family that I bought friends. I would steal from my mother's purse to buy things for others so they would like me. I was still doing it as an adult. I looked at my four children one day and realized I had never said no to any of them.

Maybe if they came to me when they were in trouble and
needed money and I said no, they wouldn't love me any
more. I was not willing to take the risk at that time.

I recall one of the louder conversations I had with my
ex-husband. He accused me of giving handouts to the children. I exploded in my defensiveness. I now realize he may
have been right. I thought I was being a good mother.

"But I Want My Kids To Have It Easier Than I Did"

In our own despair and sickness we fear the effect we
might have on our children. We do not want them to
experience the deprivation we endured, so we try to make
everything perfect for them. We who were deprived as
young children became very resourceful and ambitious. In
moderation, this is a plus. However, many of us go to the
other extreme and try to give our children everything we
didn't have. Children who are overprotected have greater
difficulty adjusting to the real world and are impossible
when it comes to making decisions. So as parents we have
to learn to moderate our behavior and attitude.

I am amazed at the number of little kids who have their
own computers and television sets. I have had people in
therapy who are absolutely devastated financially because
their kindergarten children *have* to have designer jeans or
celebrity-endorsed tennis shoes. "Everybody else has them."

I say to these parents, "I know it's difficult for you to
see that your children are dressed differently, but if you
can't afford it, you have to be honest enough to tell them.
No stories about how the store was shut when you got
there or they didn't have the right size. That's prevarica-
tion . . . lying. If you start being honest with your children at a very young age, maybe they can be normal
when it comes to money."

Jerry told me his 16-year-old son wanted a computer.
Not just any computer — an expensive model, top of the
line. His parents couldn't afford it but Johnny had seen
enough television commercials about loans, credit com-

panies and such to know it could be done — if they really wanted to.

There was a great deal of discussion. Jerry and Rita had been in marriage counseling with another therapist for quite a while and were doing well until this came up.

We talked about the reality of the debt they would incur, bearing in mind that it would soon be college time. Possibly Johnny would accept a lesser model, maybe even a used computer.

"Are you serious, Dad? Get real!"

Jerry decided that to be honest meant sharing with Johnny the difficulty involved. But Johnny responded, "You know, Dad, I've always done well at school. My grades are excellent. I'm home when I say I'll be home. I haven't been involved with drugs or alcohol — yet."

Johnny got his computer!

The fear engendered in his parents spent that money. Do you think it will end here? Not until they learn that *"No is a complete sentence."*

I realize now the damage I did to my children. At Christmas I would tell them money was tight and not to expect too much. Then I'd go out and charge, charge, charge, so Christmas morning brought a veritable cornucopia of gifts. Were they satisfied? Sometimes. Usually they wanted something else.

A normal parent in such circumstances would just say that's too bad. Dealing with the inadequacies of a marriage and also my childhood, I would be very upset and hurt and tend to lay that guilt on my children.

I know children today. I have grandchildren. I can see how a small child thinks. If I could bottle this understanding and sell it to new parents today, I'd make a fortune. I wish I had had the knowledge with my own children that I have today with my grandchildren. I hear myself say to my daughter, "But she's only seven." Basically little children are selfish. "What's going to happen to me?" "I want this." They are exposed to a whole lot of societal pressures that just manifest themselves in their demands.

When my children wanted what their brothers or sisters had, that was really normal. I didn't see it that way. I took it personally and tried to do everything I could to overcompensate, usually ending up getting very angry and delivering a lecture on how ungrateful they were. I don't think they learned a thing from that.

It's a remarkable awareness that I am getting in my later years about this kind of thing. Then people will say, "Why is it enabling children to provide just about everything?" *An enabler is an enabler is an enabler.*

Over the years I have enabled some of my children to do whatever they wanted to do without even realizing it. I can remember seeing one of my children drive his car home from school — as I assumed — and writing an absentee note the next day to cover the fact that he had skipped. One of my children is recovering, and I know without a shadow of a doubt that I enabled that addiction. I am not responsible for that young person's recovery. The acceptance of treatment in the 12-Step program is responsible for that.

When I look back over the years, I was a ping-pong ball and negotiated between children, between father and son, between father and daughter and between anyone who would come into the lives of my children and be critical. I would jump right in there and protect them. So they never really learned how to deal with other people. Because I felt they didn't have the parenting I would have liked them to have, I enabled the situation so that they became increasingly co-dependent.

As parents we have to learn the difference between co-dependency and support. Co-dependency or enabling in a parent/child relationship is the following:

- Not exerting any discipline or direction.
- Just saying everything is okay whether it is or it isn't.
- Making excuses, lying or cheating to cover for the child.
- Interfering with consequences for misbehavior at school or other settings outside the home.

To be supportive is:

- Looking at a child's creativity and wherever possible saying, "Go for it!"
- Using direction and saying, "To thine own self be true."
- Creating a spiritual awareness.
- Setting an example of healthy honesty.
- Establishing boundaries which need to be created early on.

In many ways, certainly with regard to money, I enabled my children instead of supporting them. I would provide no matter what. That was one of the errors but I knew no better. As the children got older, however, I was very supportive.

I believe my immigration to the United States from England damaged my children because I was so terribly unhappy. I had believed the move would end my money troubles and I wouldn't have to worry as I had all my life. However, the reality fell far short of what I had been promised. I was extremely depressed, lost and lonely.

My oldest daughter, then age 11, almost became the parent at that time. I was absolutely helpless. I just could not function because my homesickness was so terrible. I was separated from my two daughters for several weeks, even though I did see them every day, until we got a place of our own.

Recently my younger daughter told me about feelings she had when we came to the United States, that very first night when she was taken away from me in an entirely strange atmosphere. What was chilling and horrifying to me was that she was about the age I was when I was sent away from my mother without any explanation.

So all these things happened for me to learn to overcompensate for that loss. I learned to spend when there was no money. I learned to protect. I learned to do whatever I had to, living in this incredible fantasy of my perfect marriage and my perfect family. I didn't have it. My parents didn't have it. So I was going to produce it.

When we talk about recovery later in the book, you'll see that as a recovering mother I have created the relationship I wanted with my children. The main thing I've learned is that it will never be as I envisioned it. That's not bad. They say, "Be careful what you pray for, you just might get it." The Higher Power didn't listen to my idea of perfect relationships with my children. Instead, I now have them provided for me by means of growth, experimentation and honesty. The greatest gift we can give our children is honesty.

Learning To Say No

It's very difficult for people to stop enabling. We are confused by the challenge to be the kind of parent we are supposed to be and yet teaching our children how to survive in a healthy, loving way. I hope this book will give you some ideas.

As many popular songs reflect, relationships sometimes seem to be based on the theme of gifts, entertainment and "cash flow." I recently recalled an old English vaudeville song (well before my time, believe me!):

She was a dear little dickie bird.
Tweet, tweet, tweet, she went.
Sweetly she sang to me till all my money was spent.
She sang her song but we parted on fighting terms,
For she was one of the early birds and I was one of the worms!

And let's not forget, "Diamonds are forever." Certainly they last longer than a lot of relationships.

People have paupered themselves to show their loved ones the measure of their devotion. Someone used to such devotion can't give it up easily.

Alice's Story

Alice was such a woman. She had a lot of money in her own right, inherited from her parents. She met a wealthy man and lived with him for two years. He bought jewelry, clothes, a car — whatever Alice wanted. However, it was never enough. If she and Chester went out and she saw something she wanted, he had to buy it for her. If he didn't, his life was hell.

Chester finally girded his loins and said, "No more." The game was up — calamity!

Alice's entire life had been based on judging her worth by how much "it" cost. She could not imagine anyone refusing to buy her what she wanted. To her, a refusal of this nature was the same as a relationship ending: abandonment and rejection. It was beyond her. When Chester girded his loins even further and suggested that they separate for a while, panic set in. This beautiful woman sat in my office, told me of her fears and simply *could not get it.*

She repeated many times, "If he doesn't spend, he doesn't love." I felt I was trying to catch the wind. Her reasoning was that material possessions were critical. She had to have something to show for love to be real. It was useless to explain that if she wanted something that badly, she could buy it herself. There was no doubt that she could afford just about anything.

Even when she pressured Chester and he purchased the item, it wasn't good enough — because "I had to ask! He should have known." Not only do we have a woman who is insatiable, but she demands a mind-reader, too. "Daddy bought me whatever I wanted. I never had this trouble with Daddy."

Alice ended up in a psychiatric hospital for three months. When she came back to me, I learned she had been diagnosed as a manic depressive and was strongly medicated.

"Oh please," I groaned. When in doubt, diagnose a mental illness. Certainly there is biological depression which is frequently overlooked. No amount of therapy can resolve that without the help of some medication. However, I believe in Alice's case, this was a misdiagnosis.

Alice was an adult child from severe dysfunction. Everything was based on possessions, materialism and money her entire life. She never had to ask for any of it. That was her normal. She needed to go through an entirely new learning process to have a healthy respect for money and possessions.

Alice became very confused during her treatment. Her greatest difficulty was to comprehend the value of money and its rightful place in her life. She had to learn she was not a thing to be bought and sold to the highest bidder; her identity was not the sum total of how much was spent on her.

"How can you tell me I have the right to financial security and comfort, yet take away the amounts involved from other people that have always shown me my value?" That was a tough one indeed.

Alice was introduced to a series of self-esteem programs to help her create her own identity. She was astounded to realize her parents had bought her off rather than spend time with her when she was young. She had every piece of electronic equipment and gadgetry possible by the age of ten. Her wardrobes were specially built for her abundance of clothing. And of course, the car was there at the door, with the proverbial large bow on the top, on her 16th birthday. No expense was spared on trips, theaters, concerts, vacations, private schools and finishing school.

Alice's situation was very different from generations of inherited wealth. Her parents were not exceptionally wealthy. They worked very hard for their money and determined that Alice wouldn't have to. They overlooked the needs of their daughter on an emotional level. During our discussion, Alice could not recall one single occasion when her parents said no to anything. What had she lost that had to be restored?

1. Her enthusiasm
2. Her self-esteem
3. Her contentment
4. Her feelings of worthiness

I remember clearly the first time I said no to Alice. She sat very still, cocked her head to one side, and asked me to repeat what I had just said. I repeated, "No." She simply did not know what to do. It was like a foreign language to her. After decompressing her, I accompanied her to her car to ensure that she was all right. Within two hours, a huge basket of flowers was delivered to my office, with a note of apology attached. When she came in the following week, I thanked her for the flowers and asked why she had sent them.

"Well, it was obvious that you were angry with me. I had to do something and sending flowers felt right."

Alice and I had a long conversation about gifts and their meaning. She learned that, because a person says no or disagrees with a point of view, it does not translate into disapproval or — worse still — a promise of abandonment and rejection.

Three years later, Alice is still learning. She no longer buys gifts to placate. She demands nothing but can ask for her needs to be met — and she now knows the difference. She is in school for her business degree. She has a personal perspective on who she is and what she wants from life. And I haven't had flowers since!

Money Can't Buy Feelings

What have I learned from writing this chapter? Money, again, is not a replacement for communication and involvement. It does not help to use money to deal with feelings. As the woman quoted in an earlier chapter said, "When I broke my engagement, my father bought me a coat." That's what people tend to do.

Why did I buy so many gifts for my children at Christmas and on birthdays? Because I couldn't handle what I thought would be their disappointment. Now that I know children, I realized that certainly they want something, but they get over not having it very quickly when they get something else in its place. It's important for them to have a sense of communication with their loved ones — security, safety, a haven.

Don't take that to extremes, either to have things or to have nothing. I'm talking about a happy medium, a sense of balance which is really what people want. They may not know that actively. What they do know is when they get it, it feels really good.

What else does this cause in relationships — this enabling, this giving, this compensating and overcompensating? It creates competition. If you give, the other person is going to give you something better or more expensive.

In the relationship I have today, we buy each other silly things. On our second anniversary, because of his love affair with the country, I bought John a tape on Irish humor, some Irish marmalade and a book on Ireland. I think the whole thing cost me about $15. In the past, in my enabling days, I would have gone out and scoured the countryside to find something perfect for him. Yet I know that what I bought for our anniversary will bring him a lot of pleasure because it's fun. It is such a sense of relief when you don't have to "buy" people anymore.

Enabling is another way of protecting yourself from feeling. I know it looks as if you are protecting the other people, but in essence what you are doing is protecting yourself from the way other people feel. And, of course, aren't we all mind-readers? In relationships where people want to buy love, which is basically what *The Money Connection* is all about, they usually fall short of their desire quickly.

When I was a raving co-dependent with the few men with whom I was involved, I would go to absurd lengths to get the perfect gift. Then I would wrap it — with the right paper, of course. When I presented it my heart would pound because I was so excited. They would open it and say, "Oh, that's nice," with no feeling at all. Then I would go out and buy something else.

One man, whose relationship with me was incredibly destructive, would look at me with a smile and say, "This is very nice. Do you know what I really wanted?" That's all I had to hear. Even if it put me in debt, that's what I would do.

Remember, I had been raised in a family where nothing was good enough. People would give me double messages and, when I didn't read their minds, they would be accusatory. My mother would say, "For my birthday all I want is a card through the mail because that shows you care." If I didn't get it in the mail in time and would give it to her, she would sulk for several days. So I would go out and spend a small fortune on flowers, candy, perfume or jewelry.

I would always take flowers whenever I went to visit my former husband's stepmother. I remember her saying to my husband at that time, "Why does Yvonne keep bringing flowers? She doesn't have to do that." So I stopped. Only to hear, "She comes here every week and eats but never brings a thing." So my confusion started early in life and stayed. I would always overcompensate in order to buy these people's approval. Money and gifts are a very large part of that.

Philip's Story

Several years ago Philip came to see me about a problem with a colleague. She was obviously a gambler, an over-spender and heavily into cocaine. Philip was her supervisor. The guilt of his childhood did not permit him to fire this woman, he wanted to make her look at her responsibility to herself and what she was doing. Instead what Philip did was give her increasingly large raises.

Being a cocaine user, this woman really didn't know how to keep her mouth shut. What the drug does to you is incredible. She would tell everyone how important she was as an employee and that she had yet another increase in her salary. This was getting totally out of hand. For some reason Philip just couldn't stop.

I tried to explain to him that he was in effect enabling her. "But she does her work," he said, "so I pay her accordingly."

I looked at the schedule of increases and said, "This is accordingly? You've given this woman increases over the past three years of $30,000. How do you explain that?"

"Well, she brings in other business contracts."

I believe in rewarding, but this was ridiculous. He was not looking at the fact that she was getting all this money and was still borrowing from other people in the company. Then I made a suggestion that really frightened him. "Have you taken a look at the books lately? Have them audited."

He didn't want to touch that. I said, "I really think you should. This woman has access to funds." Sure enough there were major problems in attempting to balance the books.

One of the things against this woman was her incredible brain and her ability to organize. The cocaine was needed, in her mind, in order to keep the excitement and momentum going for her to succeed as she always had.

Like every other addict she was a conniver and a con artist who could charm the paper off the wall, and she did this with Philip. One of the things that addicts can do is sort out the people who are going to enable them. They go straight for the jugular. There was no sexual involvement here at all. It was purely and simply enabling on a financial basis.

The whole situation was getting out of control, which is why Philip came to see me. I had to make him see that he had a lot of guilt from his own past of not being fulfilled in his own relationships unless he provided for people. He was doing the same thing here and was behaving almost as a drug dealer. "How can you say that to me?" he yelled.

We soon established the fact that his self-esteem could not withstand any kind of conflict. He was very gullible as a result of his upbringing. *Everybody* in his family had been able to manipulate him since he was a child. He was born the middle child of a family of five, the other four being girls. His father was absent spiritually and emotionally. He had become the "man of the house" from a very young age and he had provided subsistence for all the women in that family. It was a very painful realization for him. His immediate question to me was, "Now what? Am I supposed to dump all my sisters, mother, aunts, all the women who are part of my family?"

My answer to that was, "That's your choice. It doesn't have to be that way. My feeling is that we can work on building your self-esteem so you don't have to physically withdraw yourself but can learn to say no."

I put him in touch with an interventionist who dealt with the work situation and also put him in touch with a male counselor and a men's group. He went through that awful phase of unpopularity that those of us who have to decompress have to endure.

"Oh, how different you are!"

"You have changed since you went to see that woman."

That lasted about 18 months. He put up with it and came through with flying colors. He became involved in a 12-Step program. His business is in fine working order now. The woman is back working for him. Her recovery is incredibly good because she realized that the risk he took meant he cared very deeply about her and her well-being. His sisters and his mother have a cohesive relationship with him. They don't spend a lot of time together. Most of their communication is by phone and they meet each other once or twice a year. His marriage is great. He's learned to say no. He's learned to be reasonable. He's learned to balance himself more than anything.

Philip had to do a tremendous amount of work on himself to learn that to give isn't always the answer. To learn to stop giving sometimes is. At all times he needs to focus on himself and look at what he's doing and what he needs in order to balance his life.

How Do We Stop Giving?

There are a lot of success stories like Philip's. Unfortunately, in the human service field, we tend to focus on less successful situations because we want help for them. I believe in every person there is that ability to recover. The Big Book of AA says some people are constitutionally incapable of recovery. I'm not sure I believe that. If you are willing to do the work, if you are willing to learn how to live without the pain and disruption, if you learn how to stop being crisis-oriented, you can have a wonderful life. I was always crisis-oriented. When Cindy Phillips, whom I respect enormously, once told me that, I was so angry I didn't talk to her for months. But she was right. Now in my recovery I don't like crisis too much. I seek serenity, peace and quiet.

How To Stop Enabling

So let's recap here. What do we need to do to become healthy and stop enabling those who really don't need to be enabled?

1. We have to examine our own behavior. What are we afraid of in terms of other people's emotions and reactions? Make a list of the fears you would have in confronting someone, in saying no to someone to whom you have always said yes.
2. Write your definition of the following: "Focusing on myself." What does that mean? Take your time on this and do it thoroughly.
3. Seek out classes, lecture series or whatever is available for you to learn some assertiveness training and communication skills. Possibly some yoga or karate would help you with self-discipline.
4. Make a list of things you would like to do for yourself that you haven't done because of the money you have spent on other people.
5. Put the items on that list in priority order.
6. Do them.
7. Look for a good support system, whether it's a men's or women's group or a 12-Step program, and make a commitment to yourself to use it regularly.

Chapter **8**

What Do We Tell Our Children?

> *We are only as sick as the secrets we keep. Sharing our fears, hopes and angers keeps open our channel to God. Never can we be fully at peace with secrets left untold.*
>
> *Each Day a New Beginning*

What should we tell our children? Keeping it simple — the truth! When we create a false image to children, we lie. Sometimes it is done in an effort to protect them from reality. We are not doing them a favor. What we are doing is protecting ourselves from what could be an embarrassing or difficult situation. It is almost impossible for a child to comprehend the imposter syndrome of its parents. What do parents do to perpetuate the "all is well" fantasy?

1. Fulfill all the requests of the child regardless of their appropriateness. For example, "I must have that kind of jeans — everybody else has them in first grade."

2. Go bonkers on holidays! "The children *must* have brand new outfits at Easter. A new wardrobe is a *must* for summer or when school starts." *Note:* The word *must* is in the same category as *should, ought to* and *have to*. These words, based on "they," are totally co-dependent. I prefer not to elucidate further. If you haven't got it, you are too deeply in denial to understand any of this!

3. On graduation, buy the kid a car. Or, worse still, get it for their 16th birthday. What nonsense! A car is a lethal weapon and, like any other potentially dangerous implement, has to be respected. Young people really need to buy their own cars and insurance. Certainly some help is acceptable, but only if the parents can comfortably afford it.

I have had more fiery disputes over this particular parental insanity than any other. I simply believe it to be completely irresponsible and unrealistic behavior. I do have a sneaky feeling that my own children had wished I was a little less adamant.

I could write an entire chapter listing all these indulgences, but I don't have to — you can easily create your own. Make a list of how many times you put yourself in hock to impress your kids — or rather your kids' friends or the friends' families. Or were you trying to impress your own family from whom you received nothing?

Honest Giving

As I've said earlier, I would warn my children over and over on holidays, birthdays and anniversaries that I was short of funds and not to expect too much. Then I charged up a storm, borrowed from the mortgage money or food money, just to see the surprised smile of wonder on their faces. Then I had to face my own wonder — "I *wonder* how I'm going to pay for all this?"

Christmas was the most ridiculous. I noticed early on that, when my children were little, they had more fun with the boxes the gifts came in than the presents themselves — which usually ended up flung in some corner. I used to laugh and promise myself I would go to the market and just buy boxes in the future. I never did but I believe they would have had a lot of fun with them. I just wasn't well enough to take that chance. I could certainly do it now.

One approaching Christmas, the first after my marital separation, three of my children were teenagers and one just over 20. I called them all together and told them I had no money to buy the way I had in the past. They smiled and said, "Sure, Mum." I protested, "I really mean it. I have a little money and I have to decide whether to buy small gifts or put the money toward food so we can be together with some friends. It has to be one or the other."

We decided on the food. That was the first holiday I can recall which was completely relaxed and totally enjoyable. On Christmas Day there were some little fun gifts under the tree, amounting to about ten dollars for all four of them. That was the first of subsequent similar celebrations. Now that things have improved, the gifts are a little more money, but not too much. I regard that particular Christmas Day as the first day I stopped lying to my children about finances.

Children need to know that the unconditional love from their parents is not based on the quantity of money spent. That way, they can begin to grasp the reality that money does not equal the amount of love in a relationship. One doesn't gauge one's self-esteem by the size of the gift given or received. When my workshop participants share reasons why they overspend for gifts, "I don't want to look cheap" and "It's expected of me" are the two that bring the most nodding heads.

How many of you reading this book were raised on the premise, "It's the thought that counts." What does that mean? The thought that you remembered to send a card or make a telephone call — or the thought of how much money it would take to be most appreciated? *Gift giving is an enormous part of money dysfunction.*

When there was a celebration of some sort for someone important in my life, I would cogitate for hours on what would be the most appropriate gift. On what was that based?

1. That it would produce an amazed "ooooh!"
2. That it was the best.
3. That I would be appreciated.
4. That all the other gifts would be set aside and my gift shown to everybody with a "Can you believe this?" thrown in for good measure.

What was I actually trying to do? I was buying respect, buying wonderment, trying to make somebody else behave in the way that would bring pleasure to me. So many times people would say to me, "You always provide the perfect gift. How do you do it?" I would respond, "I like to bring pleasure to people." But of course I wasn't that altruistic. The pleasure was what I received. That was my invest-ment. That was my identity — always doing the right thing, always providing the right thing. What a reputation!

We need to bring an air of reality into our children's lives but still let them remain children. I think sometimes parents from dysfunctional families, in their zeal to make it perfect for their children, forget that. They want their children to understand in an adult way all the things that happen and the reasons, including finances.

I remember years ago as a young parent saying, "You can always discipline your children as long as you give them a reason." I don't necessarily agree with that any-more. There are times when I've just had to say, "No — because I said so." That's perfectly all right with me now. I don't feel any guilt with that. It's really important that we create this honest interaction with children.

I have to be very careful here because I know I am writing this book for co-dependent people. I'm talking mainly to parents but also to teachers, social workers, probation officers, anyone who's involved with children. I have to say again: Honesty is definitely the best gift that you can give to children; especially when you remember that honesty is a positive word. So often the word conjures up people being *negatively* "outspoken," "blunt" or "straightforward." Honesty is also responding to the really good things that have happened in life — things to be proud of, productive methods of dealing with situations.

Starting To Change

Where do we start? There are two basic issues to consider in dealing with children. The first is that they are very logical and literal. If you tell children something, they take it literally. They work it out in their own minds. They either accept it or reject it but they are literal. An analogy would be telling a child whose grandfather has died, "We've lost Grandpa." The child is not going to rest until Grandpa is found. It's difficult enough to understand that Grandpa died. We further complicate it by trying to save the child's feelings and that doesn't work.

By the same token we hide monetary problems and behaviors. Yet we expect children to grow up normally and be able to deal with any kind of co-dependent and cash issue that happens in their lives. If they've observed us buying friendships, buying situations in business, buying education, buying status in social clubs and country clubs — then that's what they are going to do. Children are very conscious of "popularity." They're going to recognize this. We have to be very careful how we express ourselves to children.

The other issue is that, in their extreme thoughtfulness and consideration, most parents who come from dysfunctional families want to be very clear with their children and tend to give them more information than they ask for.

For example, Jimmy, age seven, asks his parents, "Where did I come from?" The parents go through the entire sex education with drawings, examples and discussions. When this is all over they look at each other, very pleased that they've actually had the courage to discuss sex with their son. Whereupon Jimmy looks at them both and says, "I thought I came from Philadelphia."

We can create mammoth confusion by answering more than the children are asking. So let's keep it simple.

I believe it is important to encourage children to have the freedom to ask questions. Yes, it gets a bit much sometimes because they have an insatiable curiosity. It is also very healthy. There are certain things you may wish not to disclose to your children. You have the right to say, "I don't wish to talk about that at this point." Be careful that the things that you are not disclosing don't come into the category of "secrets." If you are having trouble with money, if you cannot afford to buy those things your child wants, then you have to say so. Often parents make excuses about all kinds of things — "The shop was closed," "They didn't have your size," "The color was wrong," — rather than saying, "I simply can't afford it." At that point, I think it's important for the parent to feel free to explain why. Maybe other bills have come in, maybe one of the parents didn't get the raise they'd hoped for, maybe the price of something important to the family has gone up. By doing this the parents are doing two things. They are learning to deal with their own feelings of protection and wanting to spare their children any conflict. They are also teaching children healthy survival skills and reality.

The Almighty Tube

Another way of communicating with children about money is to work with them through television. One of the important influences of television is the commercials. I think it's important for parents to watch television with their children and talk about the commercials. We are currently besieged by money-lending commercials with distorted senses of false security. These commercials lead children to believe that they can fulfill any dreams because money, credit and loans are readily available. Repayment?

What's that? Percentages are not mentioned. Our children see this side. We have to introduce the reality to them. An example would be anything that compared one product to another. The bottom line was that children hate being compared to one another. The vast majority of them who came from dysfunctional families were compared to other children.

About 15 years ago, I did an experiment in a fifth-grade class. I asked the children to bring in three types of commercials: one that made them laugh, one that made them cry and one that made them angry. The ones that made them laugh were usually cartoons or just generally funny things. The ones that made them cry were often something to do with the environment, the most popular being the Native American in tears as he looks at the mess people leave in the open spaces of the country.

The ones that made them angry were so diversified I could probably write a book on all of them. Those that were competitive were number one on the list. Number two on the list were ads that put one's sex down. Those were the two most important.

The other thing they disliked and distrusted was anything that was "New and Improved" but looked the same, because they felt they were being conned.

One of the commercials that came out on top of the hate list was "ring around the collar." At that time it was always the man who had the ring around the collar and it was the woman who was so smug about getting it clean. One little girl said to me, "Did it ever occur to you that maybe he never washed his neck?" That set off a whole tirade and split the class right down the middle — boys versus girls.

We then discussed the kind of commercials they watched around holiday time dealing with toys and gifts and so on. I asked them, "What is the purpose of commercials?"

There was no hesitation. "They want our money. They want to sell the product whether we want it or not. They package it so well that we want it."

Another aspect of commercials the children noticed was the urging to purchase things to please or impress other people. They gave me a whole lot of examples like: "Show her you care by purchasing a fur coat or diamonds," "What you give to your best friend . . ." "Be the only one on your block who has . . ." They felt that was largely the way life is.

I was with these children for six weeks. We talked about their feelings on certain days of celebration when they didn't have what was being celebrated.

For example, how to deal with Father's Day or Mother's Day when they didn't have a father or a mother. They revealed how important it was, when other children were busy buying gifts for one another for holidays, that their gift was spectacular. One little girl expressed humiliation — there was no money in the family for gifts so she made some little gifts and was totally ridiculed because they didn't cost much.

How can parents help here? We can talk about commercials and what they really mean. We can talk about what is represented there. And we can teach our children choice. "If we choose to have that, we have to go without this."

There's a difficulty with children. Some want to be different and some don't. Some want to wear clothes that are almost uniform, even though they say they hate school uniforms. I advocate school uniforms, believing they do not restrict learning but enhance it. Some children go to school and compete with people who have more changes of clothes in their closets for a week than others have for a year. A child whose self-esteem is not intact will feel very inadequate in that situation.

I went to a girls' school in England to which I had won a scholarship. I was very poor, and it was humiliating to have to get my school uniform from the second-hand cupboard. But I had a uniform. Nobody ever knew that I only had one blouse and skirt. When I was in a uniform, I was proud and I was able to just get on with my work. There has been a lot of criticism for my stance in favor of uniforms but I'm still there and I'd still like to see it happen.

There's an enormous amount of shoplifting at a very early age in the United States. A great deal of the stolen products are clothing, makeup and jewelry. Society seems to believe that people shoplift so that they can sell the items and get drugs. That's not so. In my experience the vast proportion of children who shoplift take things that they can wear to look good and compete.

One evening recently I sat in front of the television set, absolutely nauseated. Rage mounted in me so strongly that I had to get up and leave. I believe I now know how a volcano feels just before exploding. It has been many years since I was moved to tears from sheer frustration. And what triggered this rage? It could have been any of the following:

1. The insanity in the Middle East over maintaining our standard of living. Apparently human lives are expendable as long as we get the right-priced oil.
2. The injustices against children.
3. The murder and mayhem occurring in our cities.
4. The strutting posturing of many politicians playing their unending games.
5. The statement on the radio that "Street people are all lazy, idle, no-good bums."
6. Ignorance, insensitivity, lying and cheating . . . *ad nauseam*.

The list is endless. But although these issues affect me, it was *none of the above*.

It was a local magazine show here in Philadelphia about teenage high-money earners. Models aged 14 to 16 were earning from $6,000 per day.

A 13-year-old tennis star will earn the following: from a skin care company — $2,000,000; from a tennis wear company — $3,500,000; from a tennis racquet company — $1,000,000.

Jealous? You bet! What I could do with that money boggles my mind. For example:

1. We could open a grieving clinic for people who have suffered terrible loss, especially the death of a child, and cannot afford a fee.
2. We could build some shelters for those people who have lost everything and have nowhere to go, who would like to work but cannot.
3. We could fund programs in psychiatric institutions so there would be no need to dump the residents onto the streets. These people are unable to function — they are ill.
4. We could start programs for single parents who have need for inpatient treatment or halfway houses, *with their children* so they do not have to go into foster homes or be endangered by a sick deranged parent.
5. We could have prevention programs, really good ones organized by people who have been frontliners in the field of dysfunctional families and know what is needed, not just those who can write grants well.
6. We could subsidize many of the programs that are not covered by insurance.

This incredible amount of money paid to young children is disgusting. Every time I see a major sports figure arguing over the "not-quite-enough millions" they are to receive, I go off again. Yes, it is a control issue. Certainly I am suffering from powerlessness. I just haven't learned how to do it yet. I keep praying for some wisdom or some direction to change the course of this craziness. Our children see, hear and absorb this.

"You Are Not What Is Spent On You"

So what do we tell the children? We tell them that you are not the price of a dollar bill. You aren't a better person or a worse person because you dress differently from other people or have less money. Then we tell them how important it is to know the value of money and to learn to be comfortable with it and how to get it.

A most remarkable book for parents is *Teach Your Child the Value of Money*, by Harold and Sandy Moe from Harsand Press. It is a *must* book for parents, beautifully and simply written. I am not going to quote from it; it is so excellent, I want you to buy it.

Another source of information is an excellent article in the March 1990 *Money* magazine called "Teaching Your Kids About Money." A representative from the National Foundation for Consumer Credit maintains that allowances should not be used to punish or reward. They say never tie allowances with chores or punishment. A family should not operate the same way as a marketplace. I'm not sure about that. My own belief is that there should be a list of chores understood and accepted by the children. Over and above that, I think it's important for them to earn their money so that they know what responsibility is.

Family meetings are extremely important here. The most successful way I've seen this happen is that the whole family meets and makes a list of things that have to be done on a weekly basis and each person decides what they will do. Then the list (in the form of a contract) is put up on the wall so children don't have to be constantly reminded of what they have to do. It's there. Instead of the parents nagging and saying, "This is what you are paid for. This is what you agreed to do," you just say, "Go look at your contract." It teaches a child a certain sense of responsibility. They can also negotiate with one another if they want to change their particular agreement for that specific time.

Most children are not taught essential money skills. A recent survey by the Joint Council on Economic Education found an appalling ignorance of monetary concepts among high school students. Apparently these young people mismanaged their money. They entered college expecting to live in the same way they lived at home. That's not going to happen. As I've said before, basic honesty, good manners or anything of that nature begins at home whether you realize it or not. The attitude toward money comes from there too.

Psychologist and school consultant Marsha Halprin of
Wilmington, Delaware, says, "Money is the last taboo
even in therapy. Lots of parents feel awkward about re-
vealing their own finances and that resistance makes the
subject seem all the more mysterious to children."

I have to agree with the writer of the *Money* article
also, who says, "Any well-stocked bookstore will find one
or two books on how to explain sex to a teenager. Try
and find one on finance." Boy, are they ever right. This
was before Harold and Sandy Moe. Buy their book!

They maintain that you need to begin very young with
everything, whether it's money, manners, behavior, listening skills, communication or social skills. Even though
it can be done in teenagers, it's difficult to reverse the
behavior of a 15-year-old when it comes to money.

Children really need hands-on experiences. I see in
schools some of the preschoolers have shops set out. I
think it is powerful that they learn how to shop. It's important that they do that and learn how to deal with small
sums of money to buy themselves things. Talking to a
small child is not enough because they have a short attention span. Keep in mind this statement from Sylvia
Charld, co-author of *Engaging Children's Minds — the Project
Approach:*

> One of the problems that younger children have diffi-
> culty with is believing that larger coins are not worth
> more than smaller ones. They believe that the bigger you
> have the more it is. You may have a hard time persuading
> a five-year-old that a nickel is worth less than a dime.

It is important to help your child save. Many banks
these days, unfortunately, don't accept little deposits but
others do. A wonderful example is the Young Americans
Bank in Denver, whose average depositor is nine years
old. Look around and see what is available in your neighborhood and encourage your children to save some of
their money. Start when they first have a small allowance
to encourage them to put some of that in a piggy bank.

As you are teaching your kids about money and encouraging them to save, you are helping create feelings of self-esteem. It really helps them to be able to save for something special that they want. I always gave annual allowance increases to my children. They didn't all get the same amount, either. The older the child, the more he got. Of course, it eventually reached its plateau. It couldn't keep on going up. That's when they started getting jobs for themselves.

One of the things few people do — and I regret that I didn't in my family — is to have family budget conferences to talk about things like going to college, what that's going to cost and what the children could do to contribute toward it. It's crucial that they are given that information to help.

I think it's important that your children have part-time work when they are old enough so they are able to contribute some of the things that are necessary. I made a deal with my son because I was working all the time and it was impossible for me to be able to shop, keep house, cook, clean and everything. He wanted to work part-time and pursue his particular interest as an artist and a writer. We agreed he would clean the house, do the wash and the food shopping and I would pay him. I offered the same amount I would pay someone to come in to do it. Because he was working and not contributing financially to the household, he refused to take that amount of money. So we came to an agreement that was acceptable to both of us. It has worked very well.

I think the important message here is that, even though you can read all these books, you have to adapt them to your own particular family needs, circumstances and agreements. That is why meetings and discussion are extremely important. The brutal truth is that you are your child's role model. If your children see you spending irresponsibly, worrying about how to repay loans, buying friendships or going out of your way to do something for someone who is not worthy of you and your time, they're going to think of that as normal behavior. While you are teaching your children practical ways of dealing with money, remember that they need to learn how to deal with money and relationships too.

Help Is Out There

At the end of the book in the bibliography is a whole list of books and resources you can get to help with your children. Don't forget to approach your own bank because usually they have some very good information for children. For example, the Fidelity Bank sends out something called "You and Money," an entire learning unit for children and parents. In it they have activity sheets to help children learn what money is, the value and cost of basic necessities, money management, inflation, supply and demand, interest rates and financial planning. It's an excellent resource.

The Federal Reserve Bank sends free of charge a list of comics: *The Story of Money, The Story of Consumer Credit, The Story of Foreign Trade and Exchange, The Story of Inflation, The Story of Checks and Electronic Payments.* All these are really informative.

While you are teaching your children the value of money, relationships and what money actually buys (which is not people or love), you are learning yourself. One of the most remarkable concepts I have learned is that, before we can teach our children, most adults have to learn for themselves first. We need to remember the mistakes we have made but not feel guilty about them. Tracing those mistakes back to our own childhood, and learning we do not have to give the same messages, is illuminating.

Remember in the chapter "The Rich And The Afflicted" how Mike was absolutely divested of any power in making decisions or feeling he could control his own environment? In this chapter I'm suggesting that we teach children from a very young age how they can get respect from money, use it wisely and accumulate it. A lot of that is learning self-esteem and how to love oneself. Isn't that something we are all trying to learn?

Take advantage of all this free literature that is available and books that are written to help children. Above all, learn to be honest. "No. I don't have that money right now because .... Maybe we can help each other save for it one day soon." Look for any other positive hopeful affirmation you can share with your child. A newsletter for children called "Kids Mean Business" by Bonnie and Noel Drew has all kinds of ideas. There is a lot of help.

My philosophy in life is that I can only take people as far as I've gone myself. In doing all this investigation and research now, I can see what is available to teach children how to deal with money. It is never too late to change young lives. I can start teaching my grandchildren how they can deal with their money.

You can make changes in your family. Take the first steps. Call the Federal Reserve Bank and ask for their series. Call your local bank and ask them what they have. If your children are living with an active addiction in the family, get them to programs just for children to help balance their self-esteem and their self-concept. The practical side of money management is being taught as the other piece of their development is being cared for.

What should we tell our children? That we love them. That they are bright, capable and lovable. That we have enough respect for them to teach them how to manage their money. That money is not a dirty word. That we all need it to survive. We can get good solid, healthy communication going. Who knows? Maybe your children will grow up to have a respect for the substance called money as well as healthy relationships.

Again, in all the practical teachings and applications, do not forget the major importance of self-esteem. Children need to understand their beauty, intelligence, abilities and lovableness. They must be taught diligently that no friendship is worth buying.

Parents might be moved, after reading this suggested material, to take it to the schools. Wouldn't that be a blast — a totally healthy upcoming generation!

9

That Was Then — De-education And New Perspectives

I'm very fortunate in being able to be the facilitator of four personal growth groups for women. I see them each week and it is very reciprocal. Working with women who are going through problems similar to what I have encountered over the years helps me to see how far I've come and helps me to bring them with me.

That Was Then

One of the things I like them to do is to take home certain slogans that we create. One is: *"That was then."* I ask them to put it on their refrigerators. Every time they find themselves getting into spending habits from the past, spending patterns of using money to overcompensate for behavior or try and stop feeling for something, they look at "That was then." It's a reminder that pattern was in the past but is no longer essential. The inner person has felt it was essential to their well-being because that's the way they were raised but . . . that was then.

I don't think men have the same kind of attitude toward money as women. I remember sitting in a Fred Pryor seminar and hearing the instructor talk about men's attitudes in a business meeting as opposed to women's. One of the issues he raised was the subject of money, self-esteem and what they were worth at dollar value. It is very difficult for a woman even to think about that. One of the new perspectives that women especially have to learn is they are worth money.

Learning to earn money is actually the first issue in compulsive spending. It is essential to relearn fundamentals—the worth of a dollar in relation to self-worth. People are embarrassed to say they want to earn money and spend it. Many never fulfill their potential as earners because of reverse snobbery.

For example, people in human services aren't supposed to have any money. (Of course, the agencies make sure that poverty remains the status quo. Whenever there is a budget problem the first people to go are the counselors.) There is the elitism of the poor built into this job. We are the problem-solvers. We are not concerned with money.

Co-dependents in the workplace are likely to experience major problems in the area of money, and much concentration is on compulsive over- or under-spending. However, there is a vicious cycle particularly for the co-dependent human service practitioner. It looks like this:

The Vicious Cycle

The professional who doesn't equate money with time usually has a problem with self-worth. Ask yourself these questions:

1. Is my client's time more valuable than my own?
2. Is it acceptable to give my time for no payment?
3. Can I choose what I do *gratis* or do I have to comply with any request for my time, regardless of monetary compensation?
4. Is my ego flattered when I am told "You are the only person who can help me — but I have no money" — so I do it anyway?
5. If you are a presenter, lecturer, trainer, do you allow organizations to wine and dine you to death when fees are discussed?
6. Do you accept that you must give your client full time in a session if they are late?
7. If so, what time do you get home at night?

8. How important is your beeper?
9. How does your stomach feel when you say no professionally?
10. Have you ever wondered — *ever at any time* — how you are going to meet your own expenses, while ministering to a client/patient/family who pleads poverty but gets drunk regularly?
11. Have you ever cut a fee for someone who smokes, goes out to eat, has vacations?
12. How do you feel, having answered these questions?

I can't tell you well enough the rage I used to feel when, having given someone a break, they then tell me that they had a party, bought new clothes, went on a weekend jaunt or bought expensive gifts for their lovers. I believe that we either retard people's growth or remove any responsibility for their actions when we allow this to happen.

People in recovery must be held accountable. If we as mental health practitioners do not implement this in our approach, we are enabling the pattern of manipulation among patients to continue and in fact strengthen.

Occasionally I have presented on this subject at various conferences.

"It was all very interesting," they tell me, "but we didn't really relate until you started talking about late clients, time and money." So many people do not connect that consistently giving time away is the same as giving money away. What's more, the IRS doesn't recognize this as expenditure. There are no exemptions for "donated time," even though it is involuntary!

An even stronger connection is time/money/work. The more time you spend at work, the more money you earn. That's the theory. Co-dependent practitioners indeed spend more time at work, but if they don't charge for their time, they don't get ahead. So they put in more hours, believing that the more they work, the more they will earn. It's all a fantasy!

I was told by a friend years ago (who remarked that I worked in ever-decreasing circles), that I could really do what I was doing and earn the same amount of money in three days. He pointed out some significant time management flaws in my work attitude and schedule. He could have been talking in Hindi for all I understood; it simply did not make sense. I was working seven days and nights a week, with a beeper, and still not having enough to make ends meet. It was crazy, in retrospect, but at that time I just believed he was being critical. So I ignored him and continued being totally frustrated, not understanding why.

What I was doing was perpetuating the established belief that human service people are here to serve. Serve what? Serve whom? People who had spent much of their actively addicted lives, wheeling and dealing, continuing that behavior with me? Right! Organizations who were out to save a buck and saw me for the patsy I was? Again—right! Coordinators who saw a person who was willing to "save people with a MESSAGE" that was me!

I believe that there are certain extenuating circumstances when I give my fellow human beings a break, but they have to prove that they need that break and that the relief that I accord them isn't going to pay for an extravagance or even another practitioner.

"I can't pay this week, Yvonne. I had to pay my psychiatrist!" Get in line, honey!!! Or "I had an invitation to a wedding and I had to buy an impressive gift. Sorry, Yvonne." That simply will not do any more. People have to make a commitment to priorities in recovery.

A couple of things give me wry amusement, again in retrospect. Have you ever noticed how many people do not show up for appointments when you tell them it's okay not to pay? Have you ever got away with this or do you pay in full for everything? I certainly paid IN FULL for therapy, treatment, whatever, even though I am in the field. Somehow "professional courtesy" never made it to my life. Have you ever taken account of your own feelings when a nonpaying patient tells you they had to buy this exclusive prom gown for their daughter? It might be a good idea at this point to put the book down and make a list of the times you have been — with your own permission — a victim of such situations, together with the feelings that went with it.

Time To Do This

Boy, I bet you are angry! When it all adds up we are talking hundreds of dollars you didn't get (and someone else did), hours of wasted time and work-load frustrations. It doesn't stop here. I have presented all over the country at various conferences and conventions as a keynote or plenary speaker, only to discover, quite by accident, though I believe it to be by my Higher Power's design, how much more other speakers received. That was then! BELIEVE ME—THAT WAS THEN!

Time for brutal truth. Most people will try to get away with paying less if they can. This goes from the private/group client to corporate management. It's almost a challenge, to see what they can get away with. People do not like this kind of honesty, but one of the greatest compliments I had was at the Atlanta Conference, U.S. Journal Training, Inc., October, 1990. A woman said to me, "You are tough, but you made me listen!" That's my personal goal: to make people listen, then act.

Why do we as professionals have so much denial in this area? Why do we reject "time is money?" No other profession does.

The fact is that in the human service field we are considered the servants of human misery. We have to be there to help, to save, to rescue. At what price?

There are people like me, self-employed, who do not earn if they do not work, who have no vacation time, sick pay, benefits. Yet we still believe that other people's needs are more important than our own.

I have had countless experiences of these situations and it was mainly due to coming to terms with the financial chaos and mismanagement in my life that brought this kind of self-imposed inequity to my attention. *I had resentments!* They were spilling over everywhere, emanating in professional jealousy, pettiness, grief and plain utter craziness. I'd be sitting with a patient and thinking, "I'm giving this person $80, and I can't afford it." That's how bad it became. Like all other recovery, I had to get sick and tired of being sick and tired. We can't forget that incredible fatigue goes along with all of this.

So what to do? I could never become the person who would not be helpful to those in need. There had to be alternatives. There were — many — but I had to do the initial work on myself. Obviously the first hurdle to be crossed was self-worth. I had to establish a set of boundaries for myself from which I could operate. That meant setting up priorities.

The first question was how much of my time am I prepared to donate? This meant compiling a list of organizations for which I would work *gratis*. Then I had to look at how many people I could see in a week, either privately or in group, *gratis*. Then I had to consider how many days I would be in the office and *no more*. These days can be flexible, according to my speaking schedule, but no more than three. I try to keep it to Monday, Tuesday, Wednesday, as they are group days, but if I miss one, I'll go in Thursday or Friday. If there is an emergency — a real one — I can be found. (The noise you might be hearing is my secretary, Lydia, screaming "Go home. It's Thursday!")

Then, having compiled these lists, I had to deal with the difficult part — implementing them. My stomach did acrobatics each time I said no. It was difficult. Talk about ambivalence. I vacillated constantly because my voices were telling me this wasn't the way human service people were supposed to be. They weren't supposed to have private lives, fun, vacations and so on. *They were meant to be available!*

However, Higher Power came to the rescue and I learned that I had choices and started to use them. Certainly, when any change of behavior takes place, there are critics. I have received my share of anonymous letters telling me how callous I am. That I'm "in it for the money." That used to hurt — now I tell people who say they've spent their money on other things and can't pay me this week, "Why don't you go to the supermarket and tell the checkout person, 'I forgot my checkbook — pay you next week' or 'I can't afford it this week, so I'll take all these groceries for free.' "

I have a very extensive referral list for people who need help. It's important for every practitioner to have this readily available. There are clinics with clinicians who have sliding scales. There are therapy groups, support groups and 12-Step groups. Help is available if there is a true commitment to oneself. Then there are extra jobs. When I first went into therapy, I was in dire straits in every way including financial. I worked to get the money. I scrimped and saved, providing for my children and I went to therapy. My priority then was as it is today: with regard to my mental/emotional health, I'll do whatever it takes! Remember, when all this was happening, I, too, was a "looking good" professional. Nobody knew the financial chaos — I put on such a front! I knew and it was killing me. With all this craziness, I was still giving time free, *gratis* and for nothing.

I had to learn my own worth! That was difficult. My worth had always been gauged by the amount I had given. Always a volunteer, asking a fee put me in an entirely different category. The kind remarks people made about me changed once I became legitimate.

Clarity here! I believe in the volunteer system. I still am a volunteer in some chosen areas. I believe in helping people out, but not at the cost of their personal dignity. My people have to give something, or sometimes I'll bill them for when they will have the money due to a job change.

What I have found interesting is that since I have become healthy and better organized, I have a contract that goes out whenever I am retained as a speaker. There are certain conditions on that contract, one of which is that I am paid my fee either before or on the date of presenting. Most people respect that clause.

Some conference organizations pay 10 days later. If that's an across-the-board policy, I'll accept it . . . reluctantly. What has amazed me is that when I really give an organization a break, I'll wait for months for that payment.

It's almost as though I'm dealing with a department of dysfunctional people who simply want to feel *powerful*.

Recently I presented at a summer school for a very prestigious college in upstate New Jersey. I went there as a favor to another colleague. It is now five months later and the tiny fee still hasn't come through. What I do receive on a regular basis is another form to complete. How do I deal with it? Realizing that I cannot change their ridiculous ways, I will not present for them again.

Budgeted Time

Budget your time as you budget your money. In the same way you budget your money for some charitable contributions, you can also do so with time for free workshops, presentations and counseling. But just so much each year and that's it!

In the area of requests for presentations from people who want me for free, I have been told, "It's great exposure for you, Yvonne." All I have known is that the exposure is great for more requests from organizations who don't want to pay either. Some very pretentious organizations (who think they are *very* prestigious) expect their invited speakers not only to present fee-less and pay their own expenses, but request that they also pay for and attend the full conference. Then there's the gracious, "We'll waive the conference fee." Gimme a break!!! I used to fall for that too. *For years.* Know what? I can now withstand the comments of being mercenary because I know differently, but they used to get me with that one. Time and time again, I might add.

I select the time I donate. There's quite a lot of it, but it is now sensibly budgeted. If it's uncomfortable at first, do it anyway. You'll start respecting yourself so much more.

Lessons From The Past

Women especially have to feel worthy to be paid their due. Our culture does not train women to feel worthy in their work. There is still a great deal of patronizing in that department — some matronizing, too. I used to say, "It's because I was raised in poverty; that's the reason I have no respect for money." What that meant was that I was stuck in the "I'm-not-worth-it" context and simply didn't know how to extricate myself. My trouble then was low self-esteem. That's the bottom line in most cases.

Even in my divorce I reported that I was "property rich and penny poor." At the settlement I wasn't even that. Naturally, I chose a man as a partner who would know all about the simplicity of manipulating a co-dependent wife. In retrospect I see it was my responsibility to confront the situation. At that time I just didn't know how.

Where did we learn all this? Where did we learn that we were not valuable? Where did we learn that money was not important? We felt we were just not worth money. Other people were much better at things and much more important. If we are still living that life, we are holding on to the past.

In recovery from anything, the past is only of value in terms of knowing how *not* to repeat negative behavior patterns. We can learn from the past so that our lives become fruitful and fulfilling. If people insist on living in the past, that past becomes both the present and the future — and disaster reigns.

Of course, it is necessary to recognize the brainwashing to which children are exposed in order to eradicate the negative behavior patterns. Reconditioning is very difficult, as children tend to believe things big people say. They also are extremely observant little things. And Lord, how they learn!

My mother took in sewing, handstitching the lapels of men's suits. It was monotonous work, hard on the eyes and the fingers. The messenger from the factory would drop off these mounds of jackets and my mother would frequently work most of the night. I don't know what she was paid, except that it wasn't very much. However, my father knew. And whatever she earned, my father de-

ducted from the housekeeping money.
What did I learn as a child? If you want to get ahead, you have to lie. What I saw was a woman who simply could not gain any ground and could not make her financial situation any easier. As fast as she got it, it was taken away. If my father bought a newspaper or gave her a few pennies to pay for food, he would deduct it the following week. And she would always have to ask for the housekeeping money — *every single week.*

When I was apprenticed at the age of 18 to a probation officer in London, my father said, "Don't get any airs. If I ever see you looking down on us, you'll know what you'll get." I didn't need any graphic details. I did not touch my potential in that job.

When I got married, I also had to ask for the housekeeping money *every single week.* I could never give a straight answer about where the money went. When the credit card bills came in, I would shudder. I was too afraid — of what I still don't really know, except that whatever I had would be taken away. (It wasn't!) My ex-husband was very ambitious. In order to avoid that possible abandonment, I signed loans, leases, mortgages and tax returns without question so he wouldn't be angry. I simply overlooked the fact that I had four children to feed and clothe.

During our separation just before the divorce, my husband said to me one day that he was concerned about me. He felt that I had a tendency to buy things I didn't need and to "Be careful, because you'll never earn as much as I do."

Oh! The lessons:

1. Do not be honest about money.
2. Do not excel at anything, as any surplus will be removed.
3. Do not try harder, because you'll never get ahead.
4. You are not as capable as others.
5. It's a competitive world and you just don't have what it takes.
6. Don't "get above your station."

There are hundreds of messages people get from their families of origin with regard to their worth. These messages continue in their adult relationships, as they usually settle for a partner whose behaviors, mannerisms and attitudes mirror those influential people of their past. These messages involve ambition, prosperity, achievement and potential. People can be emotionally crippled with such negative conditioning. Therapy can help put the correct perspective in gear.

Again, an important affirmation is needed each time one of those lousy, no-good obstructive messages comes through: *That was then.* I tell all of my patients who need it to attach this statement to their refrigerator, bathroom mirror, office desk and automobile mirror. I tell them to tape it, write it, sing it, scream it or rhyme it — or all of the above — but just do it.

That was then.

It can create a miracle. It might take a while. The changes begin in a week or so. The secret, as with all desensitizing and deprogramming, is not to analyze — just do it.

I mentioned a little earlier that in my divorce I called myself property rich and penny poor. People in general, and co-dependents in particular, need to pay special attention to the manner in which they address themselves. All that "penny poor" stuff was being fed into my subconscious. As so many people in early recovery tend to do, I had heard it somewhere and it sounded good. I hear a lot of people talk on women's issues and say they've got this big house but they can't get out. They are property rich and penny poor. The more I said it, the more I believed it. It skipped my brain and went straight into my gut. The gut doesn't have a brain. It does as it's told. All I was hearing was "I'm property rich and penny poor. Property rich and penny poor." So I stayed that way. The more I said it, the more it happened. The negativity took root and became a way of life.

"We are what we think," says Viktor Frankl. The thought translated itself into the action "Yvonne Kaye says" and there I was — broke.

Our attitude toward spending varies with the neediness we experience. It all comes from the past. How many of you have gone to a store, picked out lots of stuff and then put everything back because you felt:

1. Guilty
2. Unworthy
3. Indecisive.

Indecisive is the most powerful. That too is from the past — not being able to make up our minds whether we deserve something or not.

I used to do that, then leave the store and become very angry with myself because I didn't buy something. That also created a memory of my mother who would go shopping and come back and say, "I nearly bought you a blouse. I nearly bought you a skirt." But she never quite did it. So I picked that up too. Again, that is back to then. After I had left the store without what I wanted, I would go back and buy something else — usually for somebody else — so I didn't feel so bad. It was still spending. It was still the fix. It was actually a double fix because I was doing the co-dependent's thing and doing it for somebody else. That was my history.

This condition — self-worth according to the dollar bill — has to receive the same attention as any other co-dependency issues.

Learning What You're Worth

Genevieve's Story

Genevieve was raised in a family of boys — ten brothers. As in many European families, girls were not as important as boys. It just so happened that Genevieve was exceptionally bright. In terms of IQ she could run rings around her brothers. She had also developed a business acumen from an early age and did very well with her little schemes to earn money. Of course, she had to help her mother take care of the "men" in the family but she gave very little thought to it. One by one, the older boys all went off to the university. She was number six in the family, and the money ran out when it was time for her to think about college. She wanted to apply for scholarships but her parents said, "You'll never make it, so don't bother."

Genevieve accepted the situation as just being unfortunate. She continued her little income-producing jobs, helped her mother and enrolled part-time in a secretarial school. She made no statement when child number seven went off to college, the money miraculously reappearing for him some three years after her attempt.

Genevieve married an ambitious young bank employee and took very good care of him and their three children. As he rose in his career, it was obvious that Genevieve had to entertain and accompany him to functions of some importance. She began to feel increasingly frightened on these occasions, feeling tongue-tied, inadequate, clumsy and ignorant. Her descent into agoraphobia was rapid and her hoarding became unmanageable. She would buy no clothes or food and even hyperventilated at the thought of spending any money on doctor's visits, dentistry or vacations. She collected around her every possession she had ever owned. She would let nothing go.

In its insidious form, money had played a slow, disturbed game with Genevieve's mind. She considered herself worthless. Her messages were the following:

1. Men are more important.
2. Men are more intelligent.
3. Your worth is judged by the money available for your needs.
4. Keep everything within your own reach and you'll be safe.
5. Money is the answer to every problem.

By the time Genevieve's husband and children contacted me, they were at their wits' end. She was adamant. If it cost money to see me or anyone else, the answer was no.

So, before I could work with Genevieve, I had to work with the family.

It was the only intervention I ever did regarding money. We were dealing with an obsession here — money was a fortress to Genevieve. In her terror, she had used her intelligence — which she had forgotten — to accumulate assets and tie them up. As long as the money and possessions were safe in her hands, she would be safe.

The marriage was in jeopardy, the saving grace being that her husband was deeply and fervently in love with her. However, his work was suffering; he had reached the position of bank president and social pressures were part of that situation. The children could not bring friends to the house. Half the time they couldn't get through the door because of the "things" their mother amassed. We talked, listing the dysfunctions, the distortions, the embarrassments. Then we faced Genevieve.

At first she was totally hostile, especially toward me. Well, I was the interventionist and that is all part of the plan. I get the anger, the rage attack. She asked many times "How much is this going to cost?" I told her the fee and she paled. Then the children began their recitations, telling her how much they loved her, but they simply couldn't stay any longer as things were. The husband followed.

We were lucky. Genevieve sat there, stunned. In listing their discomforts, the family all agreed on one specific: their frustration that Genevieve couldn't see her own potential. She agreed to see me twice a week.

We worked on her agoraphobia, which we quickly discovered was not full-blown. It was actually severe anxiety due to feelings of inadequacy. After a few months we kept the discussions diligently to her famiy of origin and the messages that had been relayed to her.

We were able to identify the decisions Genevieve made as a small child in order to survive:

1. Take care of everybody and provide for their well-being.

2. Appear to take care of herself and *never* let anyone know how she felt.
3. Be totally committed and supportive to the men in her life (father and brothers).
4. Set aside her own needs and prefer death to living.

Genevieve has now reversed those decisions. It took three years of screaming, crying, loving, laughing and becoming intimate with herself. Then she:

1. Went to college.
2. Discovered what a highly intelligent woman she is.
3. Learned not to fear her own brilliance.
4. Realized that her family would not leave upon her success.
5. Has been in treatment for co-dependency.
6. Has her own thriving business.
7. Conducts seminars for small businesses.
8. Hired a cleaning lady.
9. Takes the odd course here and there.
10. Is the mentor of a women's therapy group.
11. Has learned how to play and have fun.
12. Shares the decisions about spending with her husband.
13. Checks in with me when she feels she needs to.
14. Takes vacations.
15. Estimates she has said *"That was then"* 3,689,491 times and is still counting!

Entitlement

I would think a lot of people reading about Genevieve would feel great empathy and a lot of anger. Like it or not, our culture is still caught up in this whole male/female thing. Even in the '90s there are still some families who feel their daughters don't need to go to college. Yet my argument has always been what more responsible job can you have than raising children and in dealing with their minds, their brains and their attitudes. If a woman intends to be a homemaker and raise her children, she has the crucial task of imparting knowledge to them. If college gives a person increased self-esteem, self-awareness and self-confidence, aren't those incredible gifts to pass on to children? I think so.

I also have to think of Kahlil Gibran's statement, "Children are on loan to us for 18 years." When they have moved on, it's time for the nurturing parent — still usually the mother — to do something for herself. At this point women can get into a whole lot of trouble with spending.

It is very important from all aspects of "That Was Then, De-education And New Perspectives" to see a woman in a role as educator and provider of emotional substance, direction, self-esteem and self-worth to her children. It's important because in early recovery people can get hold of a kind of anger and resentment that makes them feel they've lost something. I do get a little hard-hitting in terms of what entitlement is. If I succeed by making you really think about the next part of this chapter, I'm going to be happy.

Entitlement. Wow, can that word spell trouble! I mentioned in my book *The Child That Never Was* the experience I had at a conference for adult children of dysfunctional families. In the hallways of the hotel I was besieged by large chests covered with T-shirts reading *"It's my turn."* These people wanted to drive where they couldn't unless the car had wings. "I am entitled!" was the battle cry. My question was, "Entitled to what?" Is entitled the same as "I have a right to?"

I discovered that it wasn't. It is a distortion of "I have a right to" and that's sad, mainly because of the alienation that ensues. It is aggressive behavior for the most part, usually affecting those who are blameless. It is usually exhibited by people who cannot or will not put their anger where it belongs. If it is not targeted toward other people, then it is internalized and that doesn't help either. It's a question of who is beating up on whom. Furthermore, it is another excuse to court trouble with money. After all, what better panacea than to spend. "You owe it to your-self," the tape will run and off you go!

Certainly, if we can but center the point, there is a certain entitlement that is healthy. However, I believe most cries of "I'm entitled!" are childish foot-stamping rather than an intelligent assessment of what is realistic for people to fulfill themselves and their lives.

The reality — that scary R word — is that we cannot recoup the past. Would you really want to? Of course not. We have that most peculiar idea that if we can regain the past, we can change it. Wrong again! So you can see by now that it is necessary to let go of the past. That might take some time depending on one's tenacity. Once the past is released and forgiven, the "one day at a time" positive experience kicks in. What a joy! Initially it's frightening because we are so deeply into sabotage that feeling good is an unaccustomed sensation.

So let's make a list. (When in doubt, make a list!)

To what do co-dependent people have a right?

- Serenity
- Happiness
- Good health
- Love
- Friendship
- Acceptable working conditions
- Healthy income
- Pleasure
- Fun
- Whatever else you can think of.

That sounds good. So what's this entitlement bit? Why do I think it's unhealthy? Mainly because I find the entitle-ment people to be demanding, egocentric and damned rude. The true definition of selfish is to be healthy "of self." Self-caring is even more palatable, but whatever you call it is grand as long as it doesn't deteriorate into narcissism.

In his books *Blind Faith* and *Fatal Vision*, Joe McGinniss details the profile of the narcissist. The mythology behind this condition is of a young Greek man who looked into a pool of water and fell in love with his own reflection. Narcissism is practically untreatable. Talk about entitlement! In both these books, which are detailed accounts of true-life situations, the major characters have no definition of right or wrong except if they feel they are being deprived of something. Both these men want more, more, more — whether it is women, money or power.

My philosophy is that I am entitled to nothing at someone else's expense. *I have the right to anything I can provide for myself without harming anyone else.* Sound too simplistic? That's me — a typical addicted personality who needs a simple program for a complicated inner person.

Here's what I think of entitlement:

1. If you were born in poverty, that does not entitle you to wealth. If you can earn it — terrific.
2. If you were a victim of incest, that does not entitle you to ruin the life of any lover you might have. You do have the right to treatment and ultimately to healthy relationships.
3. If you were raised in a family where you were controlled by money, that does not entitle you to use that substance as a manipulative tool. You have the right to enjoy it and use it for your pleasure and those you love.
4. If your family did not appreciate you, that doesn't mean you are entitled to be worshipped by everybody you meet. You have the right to learn how wonderful you are, to love and like yourself. The rest will follow.
5. If you were raised in poverty, you are not entitled to spend the money of your parents/spouse/employers/ friends for your own indulgence. Neither are you entitled to have them bail you out if you cross your own financial line. You have the right to ask for help in organizing your financial life and to live well.

Sound tough? Well, I believe in tough love. It worked for me and I can't see why it can't work for everybody else.

Part of that was learning that people who cared for me didn't necessarily agree with me. I remember I used to say, "If only someone would understand. If they would take me in their arms and say 'Yes, Yvonne, you have a right to feel the way you do. You had a rotten life and it's time that good things came to you.'" What good would that have done? I mean, that's what I already thought for myself. I didn't need any help in that. I was drowning in the pity pot — doing very well and loving every minute of it — because that's what I was accustomed to.

When I was at the conference watching all these people do their thing, I saw myself. Whenever I see myself in that kind of behavior, I get uncomfortable. That tells me there's a message here. What was the message? The message was that recovery is not based on resentment and bitterness, but on self-affirmations, careful planning and taking direction from people whose opinions really matter and who are trustworthy.

That in itself is a whole therapeutic model. Learning to trust your own judgment about who you can trust is a very important step. I don't think I could have recovered without taking that step. Again, we're back to the fact that focusing on your past, on your family or on people who were negative influences is absolutely no use whatsoever. What is of value is that you've made a personal commitment to yourself.

All the things we want in our lives are reachable if we make a commitment to change. I can hear the screaming already. "Why do I have to change? After what I went through as a child!" Right. What you went through as a child. You're not a child anymore. You saw all that negative behavior. You watched your mother or your father always have something to drink or gamble with or screw around with but not have money for food or clothing or sometimes shelter. You saw all that irresponsible behavior. You told me that with your questionnaires. You told me that in your interviews. But how do you benefit by holding on to it?

Maybe the first question you need to ask yourself is, "What does entitlement mean to me?" I suggest you stop reading right now, get your paper and pencil and write down what you believe the word "entitlement" means. Then make a list of what you think you are entitled to. Once you've done that, take a careful look at your list and see which things you can provide because that's where it begins. What you can provide for yourself is going to be of exquisite worthiness. There is nothing in the world like providing for yourself monetarily, loving yourself and being able to reciprocate and communicate in healthy ways. It's all positive recovery entitlement.

There's a positive and a negative in entitlement. Only you can make the decision which one you want. Do you want to stay in the same old morass and find yourself being slowly sucked into the mud and mire? Or do you want to look at a healthy list of things well within your reach that you can achieve and feel really good about?

Each time you have a resentment, stop and think about it. Remember this very clearly: *What happened to you as a child was unconscionable but as an adult you now have choices.* One of those choices is that you don't have to be an extremist. You don't have to go from one extreme to the other of spending everything or nothing. That's just another addiction. Going through the therapeutic process or the 12-Step program on how to live with a substance called money is the best gift you can give yourself.

What We Can Change

Betty Jo's Story

Betty Jo was one of the angriest women I think I've ever met. It was just steaming out of her. The first time I met her she said, "I've got three strikes against me. I'm black, I'm a woman and I don't have a degree."

I said, "I think there are four. You don't know how to manage your money." She looked at me in astonishment.

"Oh, I never thought of that," she said.

"Well," I said, "think about it. You've had a series of disastrous relationships. You don't speak to anybody in your family. Yet you send expensive gifts to all these people at holiday times and birthdays. You've already told me that you believe the more expensive the gift you send, the more successful they think you are. Let's look at what we can change. We can't change that you are black. We could change that you are a woman — if that's what you want. There's nothing stopping you from enrolling in a college and getting a degree. Certainly you can put your money in order. Three out of four ain't bad."

The first few months of our relationship were at high volume. As I said, Betty Jo was furious. We discovered in our conversations a fifth thing that really pissed her off and that was her name. So we set about looking at what could be changed.

After two months I got her to a level of overall response that I was able to deal with. I explained to her that I was raised in a family of loud voices where nothing was said. There was verbal and sometimes physical violence. You find that an awful lot of people from dysfunctional families don't like the sound of raised voices because of the anger that's involved. In my case it was simply noise. When I am with people who have penetrating voices, my ears hurt. They physically hurt. I have to ask them to please lower their voices because I just can't stand it.

When Betty Jo could believe I was not trying to placate her, put her down or diminish her feelings in any way, she managed to tone her voice down and our communication improved notably.

I said, "First of all, tell me what you want to be called?" The name she had always loved was Sarah. That was quick. I called her Sarah. (Now she has legally changed to that name.)

Then we went down the list. I suggested that she get involved with other black women, read about black women, take an interest in her background and learn a sense of pride. Because being black was something she was just not going to be able to change. She had to learn to live with it and hopefully to become proud of it. I introduced her to several black women I knew and she responded very well.

She has a lot of white friends also. She is beginning not to notice the difference. She is looking beyond color, able to relate to her origins but also to be open and accepting enough to take in people from other backgrounds.

The issue of education was relatively simple. She enrolled in a college to study for a degree.

Then we came to the two issues of most interest to me. One was thinking that being a woman was a strike against her and the other was her money management problems.

I'd been listening to the ways Sarah addressed herself. Many times she would begin a sentence by "I know I'm not going to be able to do this, but this is what I would like. It's no good talking to me about any kind of insurance or taxes because I don't understand any of that. Women are always talked down to but I believe . . ." And this is how it would go on.

I had a sneaky feeling that somewhere in the depths Sarah had a real grasp of math. Because of her basic upbringing, it had never been addressed. In her family of origin Father had taken care of everything, and when he took off, her brother moved in. Mother never had a say about *anything* whether it was what color to paint the walls or what to spend on groceries. Sarah learned at a very early age that not only did women have no say in anything because they just couldn't make sensible decisions, but they couldn't handle money either. There was never any need to explain anything. You just signed on the dotted line.

That sparked a memory for me that I shared with her. As a child I had never known anything of the money situations in the family. That lesson caused chaos in my marriage. Whenever a tax return was completed, it was always covered and all I did was sign my name. I never knew and I do not know to this day the amount of money that was coming in when I was married. That left me with a feeling that it was just not important.

What I did with Sarah was introduce her to a woman who could explain taxes, what insurance meant, etc., and she began to learn. To even my amazement, she suddenly switched her college studies from human services to business.

Now Sarah is the vice president of a bank. Today she is proud of being a woman, of having a degree, of understanding insurance and investments. She loves the fact that she is the first black woman vice president with her bank. She is a remarkable woman. All she needed was to deal with "That was then" and undo the damage that was done. We found underneath an amazing potential her previous situation was corroding.

"I Don't Need A Lot"

Malcolm's Story

Malcolm grew up as an Army brat. He traveled to various countries with his father and the family. The Army provided everything but there was never any money. His mother was the manager and when they finally hit the United States, mother hit the casinos. There was a great deal of secrecy about her gambling.

Malcolm made himself responsible early on for his younger brother and sister. When I see the movie *Soft is the Heart of a Child*, I'm reminded of Malcolm. He was like the older child in that movie. He protected his mother from the wrath of his father. There was never any money and he felt entirely victimized and helpless.

When he grew up, he was unable to make any decisions about anything. He was never sure the person he felt he should be able to rely on would be there. It ruined relationships on an ongoing basis because there was never that trust. He refused to spend money at all. He was terrified that if the money was taken away, there would be nothing left of him.

Malcolm's mother had to be institutionalized for a period of a year. She had what I like to call a "nervous breakthrough." Even though it seemed devastating at that time, it was the best thing that could have happened to her. She went to a hospital that understood her feelings of inadequacy, her fear of being settled in one place and then suddenly being wrenched up and moved to another place and her fear that her husband would be sent to active service and she would be left with the children. She was just not prepared to be a mother in the first place. All these added things just became too much for her. She found that the excitement, the anonymity and the atmosphere of the casinos was effective in soothing her low self-esteem. It wasn't that she didn't care about her children. It was that she didn't know *how* to care about her children. So Malcolm was neither the parent nor the child and yet was both.

He grew up believing his fate was going to be the same as his mother's. He feared being hospitalized for most of his young adult life. His father wanted him to enter the military which he absolutely refused to do. Instead he became a guitarist and folk singer, much to the disgust of his father. But he told me, "I could live very simply like this. I don't need a lot so I don't worry about it. My brother and sister are well taken care of. It seems I protected them from all this hell. I am doing very well. Every so often I get this sinking, sinking agonized feeling inside of me that I'm going to lose it — so I don't want anything."

What Malcolm did was relieve himself of everything he owned except his guitar and a truck. The reason he talked to me was that he heard me speak at a meeting. He just wanted to know if he was okay. He knew that on his father's death, there would be a pretty heavy inheritance and he was prepared to divest himself of that. I referred him to a responsible counselor on the understanding that he would come and see me once a month to work on his attitude toward this inheritance. He was willing to look at this and be guided by us. By the time his father died, he was able to invest the money so he could continue his music and have a fixed income that he could live on. Whatever was left over, he could give away if he chose to. He realized that giving everything up because of his fear of money being there or not being there meant he might become a burden someday on his siblings, the state or a community. He didn't want that. Again, he had to unlearn the old message that money was bad.

Malcolm is a well-known folk singer today. He enjoys his life. He lives very simply. He doesn't mix with the high rollers and the high flyers, even though they would like him to. He is devoted to his brother and sister. His mother is now a counselor in the psychiatric hospital. I really believe that anything is possible.

There are many Genevieves, Sarahs and Malcolms. They have different names, backgrounds and problems. Understand that money dysfunction is not exclusively female, any more than any other addiction or dependency. It may manifest in a variety of ways, but basically it is the same — low self-esteem as a result of early childhood conditioning. Once that exquisite innocence is tainted, that adventurous joy of the child discounted, self-worth takes a dive. *But it is not dead.* Genevieve's method of survival was to save, collect and surround herself with inanimate objects and money. Therefore it was obvious that she had an ability to control. With Sarah, it was almost a case of reciting the Serenity Prayer and believing it. Malcolm needed to learn options and choices.

Only if you are dead can there be no recovery. Taking those survival skills, reawakening what was already inside but was sleeping, these people resolved the issues of their dysfunctional childhoods. They made healthy lives and careers from reassessing those very aptitudes that had kept them emotional prisoners. Genevieve, Sarah, Malcolm and their like can be compared to the bumblebee. Aerodynamically, it is impossible for the bumblebee to fly — but nobody told it!

I Am. Therefore I Am.

Chapter **10**

Recovery

This story might seem a little out of place at the beginning of the "Recovery" chapter. It isn't. What I have discovered beyond any doubt, both from my own recovery and from those I have worked with and interviewed, is that if there is a problem in even one area concerning money and self-esteem, that problem needs attention. Furthermore, it is usually rooted in a childhood experience.

Here's one of my stories. Maybe you'll relate.

Until quite recently, I had trouble with electricians, plumbers, mechanics, carpenters and the like. When a job was not well done or not completed to my satisfaction, I would hedge and drop hints but be completely unassertive. (Back in the '70s I taught Assertiveness Training. You teach what you need, they say!) My hints being ignored by these — usually male — authority figures, I would pay the amount in full and then boil inside. I would complain to anyone who would listen and threaten to do this and that, knowing I could do nothing.

I would feel such a failure, inept and childish. What did I fear? Did I really think these tradesmen would abandon or reject me?

Then, as it does, my Higher Power stepped in and provided me with a way of resolution. This was definitely a cash and co-dependent situation.

My son's bathtub practically fell through his bathroom floor. We had noticed water dripping into the basement. I had called in a plumber who told my son to chip off the old stuff around the shower top and replace it with new. I paid him for that advice. The water still dripped. A man who owed me money "knew about these things." As a trade-off he came in to look at the situation, which was worsening. He walked around looking here and there, making statements that were entirely foreign to me, did nothing and left.

The water continued to drip. I asked a "friend" who was a "sort-of" plumber to look at it. He promised to return. I'm glad I didn't hold my breath. Finally, when the situation was causing major concern, I called in an emergency plumber. He "fixed" the leak, "fixed" the bathtub, left a gaping hole in the wall and departed. Then he sent me a bill that would have paid for an entire new bathroom. The insurance refused to pay any of this "because I had waited too long."

I started on my old track of complaining to my son about what I was going to do. With all my "recovery," I slipped back into old passive/aggressive behavior:

1. Ignoring the bills from the plumber.
2. Ignoring the telephone calls from the plumber.

3. Returning his calls when I knew he wouldn't be there.
4. Hiding in the bedroom when he came to the front door.

One morning he caught me at home. I bravely told him I did not agree with the bill and was not satisfied with the work — it was unfinished. He countered by saying he had "quoted me a price to finish it," which angered me enough to respond that finishing it should have been done anyway. Boy, was I getting gutsy!

"Let's look at the bill now," he commanded. That male voice of authority rocked my new-found courage.

I said, "I don't have it here. I'll see you in my office at 10:30 Monday morning."

I showed up at the office at 10:00 AM. I had prepared myself. I had been told the "power color" had changed from red to yellow. I wore a yellow silk dress, pyramid earrings and affirmed my assertiveness and self-confidence. Visualizing little Yvonne sitting in my chair, I decided no one was going to take advantage of her as long as I was around.

When he walked in, I was ready. I went through the list and expressed my dissatisfaction. I was *very* organized. (He was on my turf.) He told me the very bottom line he could accept to meet his costs. I offered to write a check immediately for several hundred less than his bottom price. He took it. I was elated.

I felt good about my actions. However there was still the question about why I would experience such agonizing feelings of inadequacy in this particular area. At that time I had no idea why I was like that with storekeepers and tradespeople. I just knew something was drastically amiss. Why would I worry about them when I was assertive in so many ways? After all, I could address large conferences, lecture at the United Nations, host a radio show or appear on television. Nothing daunted me in terms of audiences, family or friends. Why tradespeople? No answer. It did not make sense.

A short time later, reading through this manuscript, I came upon the statement, "My mother knew how to bargain shop. It was always a *terrible embarrassment to me when she would haggle.*"

I recall vividly during the World War II years when rationing was stringent in England. My mother would usually take me shopping with her. She would march into the store aggressively. It was feast or famine with my mother. With some people she was a frightened lamb, with others a roaring lioness. With storekeepers she roared. She would ask for tinned pears or peaches, be told that there were none and launch the attack.

"I happen to know you gave some to Mrs. Smith," and she was off. Finally he would find her a tin of fruit just to shut her up. It is not melodramatic to say I wanted to die. I felt so ashamed when the whole store full of customers would hear this. Then when she got what she wanted, we'd move to the next store and do it all over again.

There was quite a bit of black-market activity during the war, and my mother was involved so she could then impress her family. Oh, did you think we ate the tinned peaches? Of course not. To win approval, they went to the family member most to be courted that particular week. The only time I had anything like that was when one of her family came to eat with us.

There it was, plain and simple. Another aspect of my childhood shame permitted people to get away with unacceptable work and be paid for it. I couldn't believe my good fortune. I had uncovered something snugly ensconced in my subconscious mind that accepted less.

Now that I know where it came from, it no longer is a problem. Store clerks, car sellers and plumbers — beware! I've seen the light!

Recognizing The Facade

Recovery from compulsive spending is no different from recovery from any other drug. It's going to start when we begin to look at the real pain and learn how to face it directly. You have to look the enemy straight in the eye. You have to know why it happened. It also means relearning a form of abstinence. If you have trouble spending money in the malls, stay the hell out of the malls. Abstain. Write everything you spend down in a little book to identify your specific problem areas. I'm safe in the malls for example, because I do hate shops, but every time one of those catalogs comes in the mail it goes straight into the trash. Find somebody in your life that you can trust. Give them your credit cards and let them give you an allowance. This is an addiction. We cannot do it alone.

One question we need to ask ourselves is why we buy gifts and give money when we can't afford to do so. Sometimes we are lonely and want to have friends. Sometimes we feel a need to pay everyone back. We need to understand that at times when we receive a gift a simple thank-you will do. It is hard for co-dependent people to be content with that and not rush out to buy something even costlier, something better.

Spending a whole lot of money on someone to impress them is just the same as any other co-dependent behavior. Compulsive overspenders use spending as a fix for themselves. If they buy things for other people, it's pretty obvious what they are doing. They are trying to get some kind of attention and approval. If they are doing it for themselves, they are decorating themselves because their self-esteem is so low. Underspending is sometimes harder to identify. The word frugal has a positive connotation in some areas — careful, meticulous saving. It is still dysfunctional when it is an extreme behavior.

I suppose the most critical part of all this we have to recognize to begin recovery is this facade. We cover so much of our pain and grief with the negative use of money. Years ago I managed to create a situation to convince people I had things I didn't have and was in a category where I was not.

To illustrate: About eight years ago I was driving a 1974 Comet. Someone said to me, *"In your position,* driving around in a '74 Comet! Really, Yvonne, you know, it just won't do."

When you are an untreated co-dependent, trying desperately to hide all the painful truth about yourself, you often question your own thinking. I know I questioned mine. I heard the words "In your position you *shouldn't* be driving around in a '74 Comet." I accepted that "should." So what did I do? Did I get a Honda? Did I upgrade from a '74 Comet? No — I got a Cadillac El Dorado. Could I afford the car? No! Did I promise myself every time I got another car that I would never get another Cadillac? Yes! Of course I promised. I was raised by someone who never kept a promise so I didn't know how to do it either. I just got another Cadillac. Can I afford the car today? Yes. I can pay for it. I've still got it. But I can't afford to get rid of the damn thing. It's like an albatross around my neck. However, I'm getting there.

This is the kind of thing I do. I'd do anything not to let people know of my pain, grief and major problems with money. Let me repeat that money problems carry a high degree of shame.

"People who can't handle their money are stupid." There is something wrong with that. It isn't okay to be a bright professional person but not an astute business person.

Money is simply an issue people don't understand. Just see how seductive our lives are around money — commercials, the government, get rich quick, lottery tickets, casinos — glamour and light, the whole thing. If you are not feeling good about yourself, you'll want to go where these bright lights are. Again, that's why malls are popular. There are a lot of lonely people in malls. A lot of them just sit there. A lot of them shop and buy and buy and buy.

The problem with compulsive spending is infantile. It does, after all, arise from our being deprived one way or another as children. We were children deprived of love and attention. However, we can love ourselves now. We can take responsibility for the way we feel — and we don't need to spend a fortune to feel better.

Commitment To Recovery

It is important to establish early on that making a commitment to recovery is essential. To do so means you are making a commitment to yourself. What does that entail?

1. Being rigorously honest with yourself.
2. Taking direction from trusted and proven people who know how to do what you need to learn.
3. Listening to things you don't want to hear.
4. Doing things you don't want to do.
5. Being meticulous in your recording on a daily basis.
6. Staying in the moment and moving on to another level only as instructed.

What I have learned is that this basis of recovery has to be established *before* the work can begin.

Depending on the kind of personality one has developed, the stages of recovery differ. If you have a large level of ego dysfunction, either too much or too little, taking instruction will be painful for both you and your advisor. If the arrogance outweighs the desire to recover, then this is not the time to embark on the plan that will change your life and a lot of your relationships quite rapidly.

In order to describe the process in this chapter, I will detail my own recovery. I was deeply in trouble, not knowing how sick I was. My denial was incredible. When I consider in retrospect what I did to maintain the external image of the "together woman," it amazes me. To share some of the problems I created used to cause feelings of shame. That shame no longer exists. I know I was in poor emotional health and desperate at that time. Because I have done the work, I have forgiven myself.

"I Just Don't Seem To Have Any Money"

Jane Drury of Creative Options, Orleans, Massachusetts, started me on this remarkable journey. Just imagine what she was up against — *I didn't even know I had a problem with money*. I was earning it, banking it and writing checks.

Because I never shopped in stores except for food, I saw
no problem there. Although I was still grocery shopping
for six — there were only two of us and I ate out most of
the time.

I had just picked Jane up from Philadelphia International
Airport. We had been talking on the way home about
management problems — management of one's personal
affairs. Jane is a first-class conference planner and knows
a lot about money. I hedged around the fact that I never
had time to write or do other things I wanted to do because I was always working. "I don't seem to have any
money," I quipped, "just plenty of work."

Later, sitting in my living room continuing the coversa-
tion, I found to my surprise tears were coming to my
eyes. *I never cried.* Superwomen just don't. Something
wasn't right. I trusted this woman completely, but the
issue was so deep I couldn't tell her what was wrong. She
knew anyway — Jane Drury works with people who can
earn money but don't know how to keep it.

"How serious are you about getting organized?" she
asked.

"Piece of cake," I responded. "It isn't really that bad, Jane
— I simply need to know how to deal with my money. Also
there's the little problem of not doing as much speaking
and settling down to write. But I can take care of that."

What a joke! I couldn't take care of a piggy bank. I failed
to mention some of the crazy things I was doing, like
trying to borrow money from my children, friends and
even patients.

Jane first asked to see my appointment book and checkbook. We listed all my activities — patients, lectures, train-
ings, seminars. Then we went through the checkbook and
my financial responsibilities. Nothing matched. My banking was short. I didn't think cash counted. I was about
$300 a week short of my needs. I was stunned. I simply
could not believe I needed more money to cover my monthly bills. I had overlooked the fact that I had a mountain of
accumulated debts. The lip service I was paying in terms of
decreasing the amount was a farce. I hadn't even made a

More Hours Needed To Work
8-Day Week Required

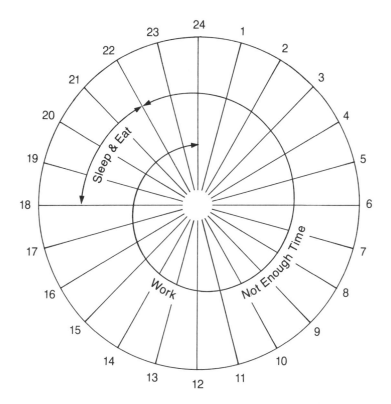

Figure 1. 24-Hour Wheel Of A Work Addict

dent. We made a list of those. It was frightening, but still I didn't get the entire picture. I thought as long as I was earning the money, the bills would take care of themselves.

"How much do you owe on credit cards?"

"I don't know."

"How many patients do you see in a week?"

"I'm not sure."

I had no answers to the questions which I should, as a professional self-employed person, have known.

"This is a mess." Jane stated the obvious — to her, still not to me. When cornered with reality I tended to withdraw and simmer. I just didn't want to talk about any of this. Jane is very astute.

She said, "Draw a large wheel with 24 segments — the hours in any day. Then fill it in with the following components: work, sleep, self-nurturing, education, play, fun, family, friends."

I started to fill it in, stopped, threw my pen aside and said, "I can't." Jane said, "Do it." This is how it looked. (See page 159.)

When I looked at the wheel, I was horrified. I cried to Jane, "But there isn't enough time! I need 36 hours in a day and eight days in a week." I saw that my life and my inability to deal with money were one and the same. It was another mask covering my low self-esteem. I burst into tears again. I was terrified at not knowing what to do — out of control.

"You have to begin by cutting back on anything that isn't absolutely necessary," said Jane. "Call the creditors. Make whatever reasonable deals you can — reasonable with regard to your own income. You must create a budget."

At this point I was almost catatonic. "Cut back? On what?"

Jane looked at the fireplace, then at the piano. When I had picked her up from the airport I told her I just wanted to stop by the florist and buy a few flowers. My living room and my office boasted beautiful flowers at a cost I have no wish to divulge even today.

"Oh, no," I wailed. "Not flowers. I always promised myself I would have fresh flowers, especially in the office, as soon as I was on my own."

"Change of plan," she said. And that was the first of many luxuries I had considered necessities that had to go.

When a person is in denial, it is deep-rooted. I truly believed the "little luxuries" were very important. In fact, what they did was hide the reality that I felt inadequate on many levels. Another mask. I had lived a lie for many years, covering my feelings by appearing to be affluent. In my pain and grief, I was totally confused. I needed guidance and direction. Looking at the wheel, I could see clearly for the first time in my life that I had no idea what looking after myself meant. I had no concept of how to say no. It seemed to me that, if I tried hard enough, I could actually be in two places at the same time. With that in mind, of course I could deal with all this chaos. How? By getting a consolidation loan! I thought Jane would jump out of her skin at that one.

"And how do you propose to repay the loan?" she queried. I hadn't got that far! In fact, I had completely overlooked that it would have to be repaid — with interest. Panic set in when I realized Jane would be returning to New England the following day. *What now?* I couldn't follow her home. I couldn't get a loan, my credit was too bad. I had no one I felt I could rely on to help me. I was lost.

Jane gave me something to think about for sure, but I wasn't convinced that my life was entirely unmanageable. What did I need? An atomic bomb with my name and bank account number on it?

The following day I drove her to the airport with a promise that I would pay attention to my accounts and create a budget. Addicts will promise anything to get people off their backs!

I tried. I wrote everything in a little book — for about a week. Then I missed a day here and there. I studied the wheel to see where I could make changes. I thought I was indispensable! I actually was stuck! I just didn't know how to do this stuff. I had been raised in a family where money was in short supply. Borrowing from Peter to pay Paul was the norm. Wheeling and dealing was normal in my childhood and my marriage. I had lived with people my entire life who lived beyond their means. I knew no other way. I regressed.

I cursed those companies that refused to "help me" with more credit (now I'm grateful to them). My favorite story of self-pity was that the wives of the prisoners I worked with used to get credit cards in the mail and I couldn't even get one when I applied. Poor me! Alas and alack! After all I did for people!

However, Jane's words had taken their toll. No longer could I make excuses about how this and that had ruined my credit. I had to take responsibility and action, but how?

Why do we have to give material things in order to be loved? We have to keep up with the Joneses and we don't love ourselves enough to be different. But what is it we are trying to fit in with? Other people's obsessions? That's part of it. The basic problem for me was, "Where did I fit in, generally?" It was difficult to remove myself from others' needs and compulsions. It was all I had ever known. I kept hearing Jane's words, would call her as a sponsor, be okay for a while and then relapse.

After this interlude, when some light was creeping into my reasoning, I discovered that in addition to the spending, my timing was chaotic. The thought had already begun when I looked at the first wheel and really believed I just could not manage on less than 36 hours a day and eight days a week. I really believed I could be in two places at the same time.

I would make lists of what had to be done and either lose a list or change it. Or I'd look at the list and add to it the following day. I would promise myself a day at home to write and then I'd pop here, do this, make calls and accomplish nothing. Not only was I accumulating debts, I was creating working confusion. I kept adding to what needed attention on a daily basis until it was entirely unmanageable. I really did need 36 hours in a day. Even that would not have been enough.

It was amazing how I fell into the whole grieving process. I can see it now so clearly — the denial and isolation, the refusing to look at the fact that monetarily my life had become unmanageable. Although I was a very public person in some ways, my private life I had totally isolated. My children would say to me, "But you earn such good money, why are you having problems?" and I couldn't answer them. I didn't know.

Then I got angry and in my recovery I went in and out of that for a long time. As we all know, the grieving process doesn't start at one end and finish at the other. You go in and out of these things. I was angry that I even had to look at this situation and at one time, working with Jane, I did become extremely angry. I didn't realize the anger was not about her but at myself and on a deeper level at the way I was raised to have this attitude of not being worthwhile.

I had no idea how to command the money to which I knew I had a right and to make the necessary investments and preparation for my older years. I finally had to face the truth. The sadness and sense of loss were put aside and replaced by total confusion. If I had to pick one feeling over and above the rest, it would be confusion. The second would be fear. I didn't know what to do. Worse still, I didn't know what I was supposed to do anything about because the denial and confusion all blended into one.

To say that I felt terror over my monetary situation is not an understatement. Here I was lost in this facade of the together, highly-qualified, personable, professional woman. Inside was a frightened little child who had no idea about how she was going to survive. In addition to that I was constantly aware of the people who relied on me, who believed I would always be there for them one way or another. My feelings of pain, grief and inadequacy over those particular relationships were monumental.

The adjustment started when I made a commitment to my own recovery. That was a long way down the road. That, too, had a certain ambivalence in my acknowledging I needed to do certain things in order to recover. I had to learn to trust myself and special others. I had to do what was necessary to level myself out — to balance. Then there was the horror of learning to say no — not to anybody else, but to myself. That was very, very difficult.

It wasn't until I started working on this that I realized how closely I followed the process of grieving, as we all do when we give up a life-long behavior pattern and have to replace it with something positive and productive. All these things were frightening to me. I've never experienced anything like it. There I was, only a few years ago, befuddled, bewildered and not sure where to start.

Everything Jane said made sense while she was with me. But I thought *she didn't really know what it was like to live my lifestyle.* After all, I was *so* in demand. That was a figment of my imagination, too. I was in demand at other people's prices or what they were willing to pay. I was not in demand in what I felt I had the right to. I didn't have sufficient self-respect or self-confidence to demand my rights or withdraw from a contract or an agreement if my needs were not met.

In retrospect, I can see how the blindness of co-dependency took over in my sickness. My patients' needs were more important than my own. I talked about feeling stuck in one-on-one counseling and wanting only to do groups. But each time someone expressed a need, I would think, "This is my bread and butter. I have to do it. I'll never be able to do anything else to earn this kind of money. After all, if I'm this important to these people, that's much more to the point than my own belief that possibly I'm heading toward burnout."

I made concessions to myself by saying, "I'm only going to the office three days a week." Then it would creep into a couple of people on the fourth day and a few people on the fifth day. Then I would say, "Well, that's just spreading it out. It gives me more time to do the other things I need to do." But in effect it didn't because I had no specific block of time. I'm both astounded and grateful that during this time my secretary, Lydia Hecker, did not annihilate me.

Then there were the organizations that wanted me to speak for nothing. They were more important than I was. Is this approval-seeking or what? Everything and everybody was much more important than I was. I still didn't know why I felt so unsettled. Now I can see why I accomplished so little. I didn't stay still long enough to do anything. The significant people in my life who were so concerned, yet powerless over my craziness, must have felt as though they were holding fly swatters and I was a large bug.

Shortly before I went into treatment for co-dependency, my colleague Thom Murgitroyde said, "It was like trying to catch the wind with you. You were all over the place. I'd grab you and sit you down. As I was talking you were up again and then I'd have to sit you on another chair and you were bouncing off the walls and nothing seemed to stick." That was true.

I had all the appearance and behavior of managing very well with everybody. I never discussed money. Never. The only time it ever came up was when I was desperate and would try to borrow some. I talked openly and freely about the addiction I was recovering from, the marriage I was recovering from, my battles as a child, getting out of the environment in which I was raised, being as I am today and wondering how I got there. I was open and honest about everything — except money.

Until Jane Drury had the courage to confront me, I never realized the desperation of my plight regarding credit, cash and co-dependency.

The Beginning Of Change

The night before going in for detox, an addict will often get very drunk or high. A farewell treat. You know what I did before I went into recovery for overspending? I said to my son, "Why don't we go food shopping and fill up the cupboards?" (There were two of us to feed.)

When I walked into my partner John's place the next day, he had taken the receipt from that spree and draped it over his television set. It must have measured six feet. We had spent $225.00 on this last splurge. And I don't even eat at home often. My last hurrah! I looked at that slip and thought, "You really are nuts. You've really got a problem here."

I'm sure by this time you have the picture of where I was in my Jekyll-and-Hyde existence. I shudder to think

where I would be without the recovery program I went
through. But I do believe in miracles. Let me state clearly:
Miracles do happen. We are promised a life beyond our wild-
est dreams in the 12-Step program. I believe that. I also
believe that a person has to be able to recognize miracles
as such for them to be fulfilled. I believe some of us have
a strange concept of miracles. We see them as the divine
presence coming down and annointing us.

My spirituality is the most definite thing in my life. It
is my stability and security. But it doesn't come with the
skies opening, the mountains parting and the seas sepa-
rating. Usually it comes through the words, actions and
behaviors of another person.

I had just entered a new relationship. John is a healthy,
normal man. He was so normal that he believed what he
saw. He saw this well-dressed, articulate, highly respected
professional woman in her Cadillac and believed her to be
real. These things didn't impress him, but he saw them.

A few months into the relationship, I asked him to take
over the business aspect of my practice. He had recently
retired from management and agreed, somewhat reluctantly at first. When he saw the mess, he was astounded
and really didn't want to be involved. He wanted to be with
me personally, to become life partners, but this was too
threatening. As a management consultant, he knew what
had to be done and did not know whether we could withstand the pressure. I was crushed. I begged and pleaded
with him. I told him I felt like an addict and that if there
were a place dealing with this money problem, I would
have signed myself in. I cried and cried (not like me at all),
promising I would follow directions if he would help me.

Finally he agreed.

The first thing he did was to create a plan. He itemized
the income and outgoing expenses and told me I would
receive two checks a month covering my needs. There
was no need to ask for any more than I was given because
for the time being, I wouldn't get it. He opened a new
business account with *two* signatures and didn't tell me
the cash card code.

I had to purchase a small notebook and write every cent I spent in it, handing it to him at the end of each week. My patients were instructed to hand their checks directly to my secretary, who recorded them and then gave them to John. I was not to touch any of them.

He then looked into the taxes, the unpaid bills from way back and created a repay system. I'm talking 1982! A new business money market account was opened, again with both our signatures.

In addition to my debts, I had to tell him how much I was handing over to some of my children. That had to be the worst part. No — what was worse was the discipline. I had virtually been on my own emotionally since I was nine. Financially, I had been entirely on my own since my divorce some 12 years previously. I had worked alone for almost 22 years, with no bosses. I never could deal with authority and here it was — *authority!*

After a few weeks of this, the honeymoon came to an end. "I work hard to earn all this money. Why can't I do what I want with it? *Nobody tells me what to do with my money!"* I screamed.

"Reasonable," John simply stated. "But as long as you are in debt, you are spending other people's money."

I began to listen, to hope. With John and Jane in my corner, there was a chance I'd get out of this alive. And well. As I was thinking this, I remembered Jane Drury's philosophy: *"Discipline is not a pejorative word — it's a freeing tool!"*

Discipline — I never had it. I didn't know what it meant except punishment. There it was — the ghost that haunted me all these years. To me, *discipline was punishment.* Another tape had to be erased.

The Rewards

I began to look differently at my life, at the feeling of excitement I felt each time a creditor was paid off. To be able to live within this plan was an accomplishment. My self-worth took an upward leap and my self-direction took on a healthier aspect. Remember, I had been in the human service field for over 30 years at this point. It takes time. I hope reading this book will help your recovery be much quicker. You have to go through the process and I didn't know that.

Discussions on expanding my work were met with common sense and support. I achieved goals I had set years ago and never even come close to until now. I had order in my life. The newsletter I always wanted became a reality. The tapes I wanted to make were made, and there will be more.

Giving over that control to another person freed me to be the creative personality I am. Giving the control — what control? *I had been out of control for my entire life.*

At this point I recalled a visit Jane and I had made to Bill Wilson's grave. It had been hard to find because it was ordinary. I expected acknowledgment of his amazing gift to the world — Alcoholics Anonymous. The only acknowledgment was the collection of cards, letters and prayers at his headstone. I experienced such a strong surge of humility at that grave that day, it brought me to my knees. It was a spiritual awakening that changed my perception of life.

It is said that the Higher Power works in strange ways. I agreed. I believe my visit to that grave prepared me for the humility it took to get my life in order. I'm a PAC woman — Pride, Arrogance and Control — in the negative sense. They damn near killed me. Now I have channeled them to be productive parts of my life. My humility allowed me to take direction from others who knew better than I did and still do. I still have my two checks a month. This is the first year my tax returns have been on time. I have broken the back of outstanding debts and loans. I might even get a raise — when they are all settled.

This is how my wheel looks today.

In the beginning it is important to do a daily wheel. Even now, if my timing is off and I start complaining that I don't have enough time, I do a daily wheel. Those I have reproduced here are somewhat generic.

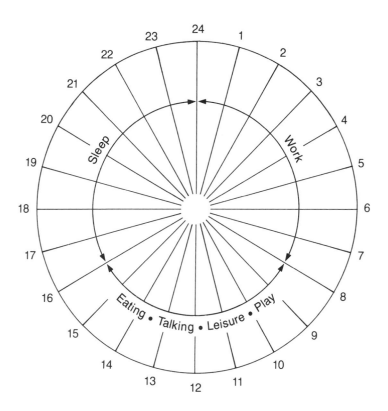

Figure 2. Ideal Balanced 24-Hour Wheel

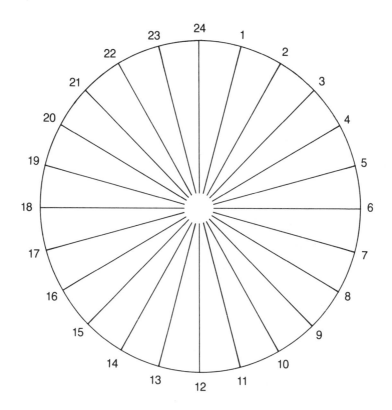

Figure 3. Your 24-Hour Wheel

(Photocopy and complete one every day for a month. Then evaluate.)

The Recovery Process

Let's look at what we need to do as we move toward creating a manageable financial life.

1. Get a notebook and write down *every* expenditure.
2. Get another notebook and record your *actual* time schedule.
3. Recognize your "place" problem and keep away from:
   a. Malls
   b. Shopping centers
   c. Discount houses
   d. Casinos
   e. Race tracks
4. File the catalogs in the trash bin.
5. Don't watch the shoppers' channels.
6. Go to:
   a. Debtors Anonymous
   b. Overspenders Anonymous
   c. Shoppers Anonymous
   d. Gamblers Anonymous
   e. Gam-Anon
7. Talk to a friend when you feel the urge to go spend.
8. Hand over your credit cards to a trustworthy person.
9. Learn to budget with the help of a financially astute friend or hire someone. (See Appendix I.)
10. Negotiate with your creditors. They only get mad when you ignore them.
11. Use cash. If you haven't the cash, you can't afford it.
12. Do not get new loans to cover existing debts.
13. Do not borrow on life insurance.
14. Do not juggle your money from one bill to another.
15. Do not use credit cards to finance each other.
16. Learn to say no with love.

It works. It may look as if I've just opted out of your solution, but *you* have to keep on doing it. *It works!* Find the root of the problem, examine your self-esteem and the rest will take care of itself. God knows, there are enough people out there willing to help you to get back into action and get spending. American advertising is our enemy — it loves the Joneses. But they cannot help you with the way you look at you or the way you feel about yourself. You must learn to look at your own beauty.

An excellent book which is a *must* (yes, even though that's on the forbidden vocabulary list) for overspenders is *How to Get Out of Debt, Stay Out of Debt and Live Prosperously*, by Jerrold Mundis (Bantam Books). Excellently compiled, with humor and sound common sense, it really shows you "how to."

Keep a journal. Write it down. But don't compare yourself to anyone but you. Then look back. Journals are wonderful things because you can look back and say: "That's where I was then. Look where I am now."

How exciting! Look within. If you're not sure, ask somebody, "What do you see in me?"

Don't be afraid of letting someone know you. If you can't let them in, at least work on yourself so you can come out. Then you will be able to reach out and accept some help.

Trash those insidious offers that come in the mail. Don't even look at them. If necessary, have a family member toss them before you even see them.

There are groups for compulsive spenders now. Shoppers/Overspenders/Debtors Anonymous — take advantage of them. You have the right to feel good about you. What you have is a compulsion of some kind. To love yourself is the basis of all recovery regardless of the problem.

With all this work done on organizing money, budgets, repayments and dealing with debts and creditors, let's not forget time management. It is essential to recover from this chaos.

Rewards are essential, too. Don't let us lose sight of the fact that in recovery from monetary problems there's a need for your progress to be recognized. It is serious business, true. At times it is very painful learning to separate the child from the adult. Strengthening the adult to take care of the hurting child, to nourish, to nurture, to care for it is critical here. One of my mottoes is: *Life is grim but not necessarily serious.* It is part of healthy living to be able to intersperse recovery with fun, laughter, treats and rewards. I believe we need to recognize each stage of accomplishment. So often in the invisibility of our growing years, nothing positive was recognized. Because so much of our painful co-dependency is tied up with those behavior patterns, we don't give ourselves the support and caring to which we have a right.

Following instructions from whoever becomes your advisor is important to you and your well-being. Those instructions include careful planning. In order to recover from compulsive spending, you need a plan. You need an order to things. You need structure where there has been none. Above all, you need long-term and short-term goals.

If you want further information in regard to goal-setting, you can do no better than to go to your library and borrow tapes from the great motivators such as Fred Pryor, Dennis Waitley and Napoleon Hill. I think it is good to own some of these tapes, but not while you are repaying a debt that is awaiting your intention. Use the free library for now. When things get better, you can purchase whatever you want.

Goal-setting is very important because it gives us something to look forward to. There are specific ways to set goals and they need to be discussed with your advisor to maintain a realistic perspective. Sometimes when we owe a lot of money, we want to get together the amount and pay one thing off completely. That's not always wise. I remember feeling so proud of myself that I had a money market account and saying to John one day, "Isn't this wonderful? I have a money market account. I'm doing so well."

He said, "Yes, that's great but look at what you owe. You're earning seven percent in your money market account and your credit cards are charging you between 15 and 18 percent on what you owe."

This is what I mean about talking with people who are familiar with these details. If you don't have a financial brain, you can get one. If it isn't yours, then use someone else's until yours is trained. A consumer credit organization can be of enormous help. The 12-Step program is invaluable here also.

Keep your goals simple. Make a list of them. Have two lists specifically of long-term and short-term goals. Short-term goals could be similar to the following:

1. I want to complete this job by X amount of time.
2. I want to pay off this credit card by X amount of time.

Each time you accomplish a step that really is firm and there is a change, then it's time to reward yourself.

I listened recently to a tape by Dennis Waitley on the subject of writing a book. He plans his time for each stage of the work, and when he finishes a stage, he rewards himself. He will do a variety of things. He might go out for a walk that he's never given himself time to do. Then when he gets to the next stage, maybe he'll go out to dinner with his wife. Once the book is completed and at the publishers, they'll go away for a couple of days. These are the kinds of things that give him not only goals to accomplish his work, but rewards to look forward to.

I haven't had a really good vacation in years. Part of my recovery process is to work for an amount of time and then set a few days aside at regular intervals, maybe three or four times a year, to go away. Then once a year I plan to have a proper vacation — to go back to England maybe or see other parts of the United States — something I feel I have truly earned. When we are dealing with monetary issues, I do believe rewards are important. Those rewards should be financial ones only when we can afford them.

Looking at my goal of having repaid debts and so on, I would get to various levels of my goal. Then I would feel I had accomplished something and I could allow myself some kind of rest and relaxation.

Kay Fogg, a dear friend, offered me the use of her house in the mountains to finish this book (another goal). I remember saying to her, "I don't want to break another leg." In writing my first book, *The Child That Never Was*, I broke my leg because I just wouldn't set enough time aside to finish that book. This time I got smarter. I went away to the peace and quiet of her home in the mountains and completed the book. For me that was an accomplishment, but it was also a reward. I allowed myself time to go and consolidate my efforts, which is something I would never have done before.

Celebrate Yourself!

Being a crisis-oriented person, it fed my egocentricity and grandiosity to say, "I don't know how I got this book written — I just have an hour here and a couple of hours there. Look what I did!" That's foolishness! I know that now. It's very important that we celebrate ourselves in our recovery. Recovery from monetary issues is more than declaring character defects constantly.

At the end of this chapter are The 12 Steps Of The Adult Children Of Dysfunctional Parents, which I wrote to accommodate the hurt child. See how gentle they are? It is harmful to keep remembering the things we did, putting ourselves down, calling ourselves stupid or inadequate and perpetuating a myth that people who have money troubles are fools. That isn't so. People who have money troubles carry a heavy burden of shame. It's very difficult for them to share this even in a meeting. Thank God, Shoppers Anonymous, Overspenders Anonymous and Debtors Anonymous are beginning to come to the forefront now. We are recognizing that this is indeed a widespread problem. (The parent of us all, the government, is more in debt than anybody. What a frightening role model that is.)

We all need affirming. Too often we have looked in the wrong places or to the wrong people to seek the validation that has to come from within us. If you give the power of affirmations to another person, and that person leaves and takes the affirming with them, what do you have? A bereft co-dependent person.

A final and crucial part of my recovery is my "God Bag." Someone I love very much told me about the God Bag. All I do is write a letter to God and say, "I can't handle all of this stuff on this list." (I always give my Higher Power a list.) I say, "I just can't deal with it," and into the bag it goes. It's amazing. As I put problems in that bag and zip it up, I turn them over to God. And I am given solutions. I also have a God Box in the office. Start a God Box and turn your worst spending problems over to God. It works. Just be sure you know what your real problems are first and ask for strength, courage and guidance to implement the recovery process, using the given tools.

If any of this sounds oversimplified to you, please go back to the beginning of the chapter and read it again. This has been a long, arduous journey and I'm still on the path of recovery, even though now I am at the stage where it is exciting and rewarding. Daily living problems still arise constantly. When people are in trouble and need help, what do we do? The intricacies of our brains can get us into so much trouble. At this point we really need the strength of the 12-Step program, a sponsor, a manager, an advisor or a trusted friend before we do anything. I can remember going to a store in the early stages of my recovery and being really petrified. I simply did not know how to spend or how not to spend. I just asked very simply, "Would you please come with me?" and a friend accompanied me. All I had to do was ask. So keeping it simple is an excellent philosophy, especially when we are dealing with such a complex problem.

The major part of the recovery process is to be in the company of people who can be objective, and can get to the root of the problem and simplify it. If we think we can do it ourselves, especially in this particular area, then we have fools for advisors. It isn't just a question of objectivity and support here, it is being with people who are knowledgeable. A combination of a business brain plus the 12-Step philosophy, therapy and recovery from child-hood issues is all essential.

Whatever it takes — you need it all!

And remember:

If you spend money unnecessarily when you still have debts, you are spending other people's money.

—John Aar

Discipline is not a pejorative word — it is a freeing tool.

—Jane Drury

The 12 Steps Of
The Adult Children Of Dysfunctional Parents

1. We admitted that we were powerless over our parents, their dysfunction and behavior.

2. We came to believe that a Higher Power who was connected to the child within us could restore us to sanity.

3. We made a decision to turn our will over to our Higher Power and to stop the enabling and fixing we had utilized in the past.

4. We took time to look gently within, without judgment or fear.

5. We shared our discovery with another human being and our Higher Power.

6. We communicated with our Higher Power and asked for guidance in using the tools given us to remedy our poor self-esteem and self-image.

7. We examined our negative attitudes and learned how to replace them with positive thoughts and behavior. We learned to trust and enjoy our good feelings, rather than to fear them.

8. We made a list of all people who were positive and honest in our lives. We resolved to discuss with those people any problem or negative projections that would put us back in the fearful frame of mind from which we are growing in beauty and love.

9. Observing our changes, those close to us become concerned and afraid. We will immediately make direct amends to those we hurt, so that we will no longer accumulate a slush fund of guilt, pain and anger as we have in the past.

10. We continued to grow in self-worth and universal love and acceptance of ourselves and all those who

encourage us. We learn to recognize and nurture the child within.

11. We sought through prayer and meditation with our Higher Power, and open dialogue with those whom we love and trust, to nurture, hold, love and protect the little child within us. To guide, support and love unconditionally, so that we can become productive, warm, capable and loving human beings.

12. We share our spiritual awakening with others. Acknowledging the love of our Higher Power which dwells within us, we are messengers of hope to those who are now suffering in the way we once were, before we found each other. We resolve to practice these steps in all our affairs, for when we give love away, it becomes the best part of our being.

Adapted from *The 12 Steps
of Alcoholics Anonymous.*

Chapter 11

The Miracle Of Affirmations

Because of our negative conditioning it is difficult to affirm ourselves. Co-dependents are the combination of what everybody else wants them to be — so where is the identity to affirm?

This whole self-image thing can get royally screwed up. I used to ask myself what the problem was when people would say they couldn't afford me and become enraged if I didn't take responsibility for their situation.

One man told me, "Yvonne, everybody thinks you're rich!" I protested, knowing this

181

is not so. When I shared it with a friend, she said, "Let 'em think it. Maybe it will rub off on you."

That was then. Now I affirm myself and have recovered from the poverty syndrome.

Affirmations are miraculous. The most important aspect of affirmations is that *you don't have to believe them, just state them.*

We have been shown in so many ways how effective repetition is. The 12-Step programs all use slogans, one-liners and prayers. It is obvious how effective repetition is when we consider the negative things we heard in our formative years and came not only to believe but to live. As small children we created our own survival skills. We have to acknowledge that they were probably the wrong decisions. Nevertheless, they worked at the time. In treatment an effort is made to raise those memories from the unconscious, face them and reverse them. This means coming to terms with the reasons for the decisions and releasing them.

Along with this activity is the need to delve into the messages that were given to us as children, both verbally and non-verbally. A lot of those messages have already been recorded in this book.

Take a few moments now to sit quietly with paper and pencil and remember some of the messages you received regarding money when you were growing up. Not necessarily just what you saw in your family but what you heard, possibly including some double messages. They can only come from you. So do take some time to do that now.

You might wonder why it's so necessary to recall such painful past experience. My feeling is that the pain cannot be erased and the decisions cannot be reversed *until they are recognized.* Many people report that they have put the past behind them and they are fine. We all know what *fine* stands for. I tend to think there is a possibility some people can do that. They can just shut their mind down and get on with today. If that is genuine, it's wonderful but the vast majority of us can't. There's that nagging feeling in the pit of our stomachs when a situation occurs that triggers a feeling or a memory and we don't really know what it is on a conscious level. Until those memories are eradicated, the mistakes will continue, the lifestyle will remain unchanged and the potential will never be reached.

Creating Your Own Affirmations

Affirmations are tools for recovery. They are deeply personal. They cost nothing except a little of your time. Repetition is essential. How do you write your own affirmations? One effective way is to sit quietly for a little while and consider your current life situation. What are the people, places and things that cause you pain, grief or discomfort? Make a list of them. On that list can be things such as feeling unfulfilled in your job, not having a good relationship with important people in your life or feeling that you have little confidence. Make the list and then make a second list beside each one of what would be its opposite.

There are certain important aspects of creating affirmations. I think it is critical to focus on yourself. Having affirmations to change other people or other circumstances doesn't usually work but to affirm oneself is important. Bear that in mind as you again look at the lists you have created. Put them in priority order according to your needs. They can cover anything and everything in your life. Let me give you a few examples:

1. I affirm my comfort and security with the substance called money.
2. I affirm my time-management skills.
3. I affirm my business acumen.
4. I affirm my potential, personally and professionally.
5. I affirm my financial security and comfort with joy and pleasure.
6. I affirm my excellent mental, physical, spiritual and emotional self.

7. I affirm my creativity.

8. I affirm my ability to earn an excellent salary.

9. I affirm my contentment, acceptance, honesty and serenity.

10. I affirm the joyfulness in my life.

11. I affirm my success as a writer, lecturer and trainer.

12. I affirm my reciprocal love with my life partner.

13. I affirm my prosperity and abundance of money.

14. I affirm my dignity, composure and confidence in all financial matters.

Continue the list and create your own. These do not always have to be said all the time. The affirmations are whatever is necessary for the period of time that you require support.

Let me repeat: *You don't have to believe it, you just have to say it.*

Before I even repeat affirmations, I affirm myself as a beloved child of my Higher Power. Never having had a tight family unit in my childhood, I have created one by being a child of the universe. I also pray for the will to will Its Will — "It" being my Higher Power.

There are many excellent books on affirmations. Some of my special favorites are listed in the bibliography. I read one or two of them every day, depending on which part of me is in need of support — the child within or the woman.

Why Affirmations Work

In the human being, there is a constant battle between the power of the brain and the position of the subconscious. The subconscious does not have a brain. It does as it's told. It's extremely important that we feed positive data into the brain to be transmitted into the subconscious because the subconscious acts upon its instruction. When we were little, the data fed into our brain was negative. It was confusing, and it was a double message. Our little brains just could not comprehend it. We could make no sense of it. So we either hid from it or acted out on it, but we certainly didn't deal with it.

What we have to do now as adults is be consciously aware of what we feed into our subconscious. In Viktor Frankl's book *Man's Search For Meaning*, he states that people make conscious decisions about the way they feel.

I remember going to a retreat quite a while ago and hearing the retreat master say people make a choice to love. I was furious at hearing that because in my unhealthy relationships I felt totally out of control. I felt I had no choice at all and would just "become infatuated," "fall in love," or whatever. I realize now that I have a choice in everything, including how long I dwell on issues, how long it takes me to invoke the Serenity Prayer and really take a look at that over which I have control and that which I don't.

For a controller, as so many of us are, affirmations are extremely difficult to begin with. I wanted to see results immediately. In the same slow way the corrosion took place in our growing years, the diffusion of all those old negative jaded messages takes time. The best way to erase the tape is to tape over it. Affirmations are positive methods of retaping over old dangerous messages. Your brain will start telling you, "Look, this isn't going to work. Where did you get this idea that you can just affirm something and it's going to happen? Why bother? I mean, you've been doing it for a week — have you seen any change?" No, of course not.

However, as an adult you can say to your brain, "Just do it. Don't think about it, just do it." Believe me, affirmations grow on you. After a while they are an automatic reaction to a crisis, an automatic repetition of something that begins to diffuse the tension and the stress.

I have to remember at all times that I am still a controller. When a situation occurs at a national or international level which will affect my life and I have absolutely no control or influence whatsoever, I do a royal number on myself until someone in my life whose opinion matters tells me to stop worrying because there is nothing I can do about it. If there really is nothing I can do about it, I do my best to affirm myself to reaffirm my faith, however uncomfortable that may be, and in a short space of time I begin to feel better.

One of the snags in using affirmations is that, like prayer, we don't always get the results we envision. Far too often I've picked up the 12 Steps and 12 Traditions or I've used Rune stones for a reading only to be told, "Will you get out of your own way, Yvonne?" That applies to success, financial matters, realizing one's own potential or being creative. When we are dealing with co-dependency, we are frequently in our own way. When we are dealing with co-dependency and the misuse of money, then not only are we in our own way but we are also in the driver's seat, very much in danger of running ourselves over.

It is essential in recovery that with all the other practical applications, we use affirmations if for no other reason than to erase the old messages. We need to get rid of those virulent, intrusive voices that come to us when we are attempting something new or adventurous — the ones that say: "You'll never make it." "It costs too much." "What makes you think you can do that?" "You'll never afford it." "That's a rich person's occupation." "Better people than you have tried that."

Affirmations can silence those voices.

There's a difference between affirmations and prayer, although there are similarities. Affirmations are basically looking at the capabilities and talents that we already have and affirming them. The only way people do not realize and fulfill their abilities is because the little voice is saying, "You can't."

Keeping it simple is a prerequisite for successful affirmations. Once the affirmation gets complicated it gets too fuddled and doesn't work. It's a question of making the repetition and then setting it aside — just getting on with your life. This is where the control factor of the co-dependent has to be in control of itself. If it's trying to make the affirmations work by putting energy toward them, rather than just doing them in the method prescribed, then frustration will ensue.

Some of the books on affirmations are absolutely beautifully written. The prose is exquisite, almost poetry. That is good to read. Our affirmations don't have to be that way. They can be very, very simple. Just one-liners: "I affirm myself." I say that a lot. When things happen over which I have no control and I begin to doubt myself, I affirm myself. *Sometimes I accept myself.* "I affirm that I am lovable and capable." Remember what is important:

1. Affirmations must be repeated on a daily basis.
2. Affirmations must focus on you, not on other people in your life.
3. Affirmations do not have to be believed, just stated.
4. If anything troubles you, write it down and affirm the opposite.

Just let me pick out one thing from that list, affirming yourself and what is in your life. The affirmations have to come from *"I affirm for me."* It is not acceptable to affirm somebody else's success, good health or creativity. If you want to do that, there's another way: Suggest that people in your life do their own affirmations and show them how to do it. Some of them are going to be very resistant but that's okay. I have bought daily affirmation books as gifts for people I care about. I know some of them read their book every day, some read it sporadically and some don't read it at all.

I refer to affirmation books as magic books because they always seem to say what I need to hear on that particular day. Really — it's magic. The affirmations, therefore, are for yourself. If you have concerns for other people, let me share with you what I do.

Every day when I wake up the first thing I say to myself is the Serenity Prayer followed by, "I affirm that I am a beloved child of my Higher Power." Then I go through whatever affirmations I need for that day. Then I visualize myself in the pure light of protection, usually surrounded by the divine healing color of emerald green, and everybody I care about is in that light with me. Furthermore, I see the arrows of negativity from the outside world coming at me and bouncing off that protective layer out into the universe. On a day-to-day basis I am in that bubble, aura or protective shield. It always has to be my self first — always — and with me is my life partner, my children, the beloved people in their lives, my close friends.

If any of those people are experiencing some severe problem, I will then visualize them in their own light and their own protection so it is very strong. In addition if there are problems of national urgency and importance, I will put the leaders of various communities, states or countries in their divine light, send blessings to them and turn them over to the Higher Power. I do not affirm for these people; I just whip a strong field of energy around them. We are all capable of doing this. Like love, the more of this positive energy that you give away, the more you get back.

Do your affirmations now before you read anymore. Create them, make a list of them and start saying them. It doesn't have to be as soon as you wake up in the morning — it can be morning, noon, night, driving around in a car or any time. I do believe that I am what I think. If I think positive affirmations frequently, then that improves and enhances my life.

People sometimes say when they are very successful, "I just don't know how this happened." I say the same myself. The more I think about it, the more I believe that faith, affirmations, prayer, belief in a Higher Power and being able to listen to options and alternatives from people I trust are all responsible for whatever has happened for my highest good in my life.

People often say to me when I talk about affirmations, "How can you account for the terrible things that happen in people's lives?" I can't account for that. All I know is that it is more productive to think positively than negatively. It is more productive to project affirmations than to worry about things beyond my control. Let me add this to clarify the situation. Affirmations are powerful. That does not mean using them will make a person's life totally problem-free. It doesn't mean they will be without concerns, sometimes even tragedies. There is nothing as constant as change. The fact remains that sometimes all we have is faith. Affirmations are a large part of faith.

Remember when you are making your affirmations that one of the reasons you got into trouble with money was that you didn't recognize its value in your life. You didn't recognize *your* value in your life. Some of you, like me, were afraid and even ashamed of wanting money. So if one of your affirmations is, "I affirm that I am wealthy," go right ahead. Remember, while you are affirming, to look at the practical application too. Look at your budget, your organizational skills, what needs to be done and affirm all the time. While you are working on that, you affirm.

In my recovery, having to learn about possible investments, percentages, gross, net, taxes — all these things that I had absolutely no concept of in the past — was enhanced by affirming my ability to do all those things. I believe that, although I have organized my life in such a way that certain people take care of certain things, should it be necessary I would be able to take care of my finances. That is due entirely to my belief that the combination of practical application — learning and education — with daily affirmations spells recovery.

Nobody ever made any rules to state you are a better person when you are poor. Learning to live with financial security is a wonderful involvement.

I spent a lot of years trying to be different from my mother and I ended up just like her — broke. Until I recognized the reasons and was able to release them, I did all the things she did. She did what she did to be accepted in the middle of 13 children. She didn't want to be a nothing. I inherited that.

The only person you really have to please is yourself. Once you please yourself, everybody else will fall magically into line. No matter if the problem is spending, drugs, alcohol, sex, food, work or whatever, learning to love yourself is the basic ingredient in recovery. That way serenity lives.

Chapter **12**

Where To
From Here?

Where indeed! This chapter is largely a figment of my imagination. Apart from support groups, a few knowledgeable financial consultants and money management courses, there is little available for recovery from money issues. Many groups are powerfully effective, yet not sufficiently well-known: Debtors Anonymous, Overspenders Anonymous and Shoppers Anonymous. Look up the information under Self-Help Groups in your local phone directory. If these programs are not readily accessible, go to Co-dependents Anonymous, or if you have another dependency, go to the appropriate 12-Step meetings. Here are some resources I have found:

1. Debtors Anonymous
   General Services
   P.O. Box 20322
   New York, NY 10025-9992
   212-642-8222
   Very confidential
2. The National Foundation for Consumer Credit
   8701 Georgia Ave., Suite 507
   Silver Spring, MD 20910
   800-388-2227
      This organization will give you information regarding your local chapters. There is no fee and they are exceptionally helpful in debt-paying and structure.
3. Creative Professional Planning
   Jane Drury
   P.O. Box 413
   Orleans, MA 02653
   508-255-5869
4. Toni Severns
   215-637-2595

Both Drury and Severns are well versed in budgeting, together with co-dependency and why people get into such financial chaos. It isn't a question of simple money management, it's how to maintain a high level of self-esteem and know that one does not have to buy it. Look in your own neighborhood for advisors and check them out carefully.

Treatment

I would like to see questions on spending habits added to the assessment of patients admitted to inpatient addiction and co-dependency treatment centers. This is especially important in eating disorder facilities, as there appears to be a cross-dependency with food and money. In addition, should discussions around money arise, therapists need to be aware of the relapse potential if this condition is discounted. (Excuse the pun—I am recovering, after all!)

Training And Education

Training must be available, indeed mandated, for CAC counselors, therapists, psychologists and psychiatrists to recognize monetary problem areas.

Alternative education and training must be presented to the judiciary, probation departments, children and youth and social services departments. We are looking at a severe crisis in view of the seductive advertising to which people are exposed. In time, I envisage components of inpatient programs being dedicated to "Credit, Cash and Co-dependency."

As an aftercare plan, attendance at "How To Deal With Your Money" classes would be essential. Together with work on self-esteem and self-confidence, this would provide a practical basis of recovery, some structure and a plan.

The use of money coupled with self-esteem should be a required course for teachers, especially at grade school level. *Note:* This is not a "How To Handle Your Money" course alone. *It must be incorporated with self-worth and self-esteem.* This aspect can be promoted by using the following tools:

1. Discussion groups on the subjects of:
   a. Friendship
   b. Family
   c. Relationships
   d. Sexuality
2. Pride in accomplishments
3. Goal-setting
4. Teaching students to be comfortable with money, the importance of it and how to use it for their highest good.

Kaye

5. Special attention to TV commercials—quick loans, quick wins, quick money, quick resolutions.

Senior high school students need this information. A class dedicated to "Messages In Commercials" at any age is remarkably informative.

Business

Awareness courses should be available to Employee Assistance Programs and all management levels on confrontation techniques. Many overspenders are potentially fraudulent. Asking for salary advances, borrowing from colleagues or absences from work on a consistent basis could add up to a problem spender. The self-esteem aspect means an employee's personal appearance and behavior might change. Look for high tension and additional stress factors.

The 12-Step program and support groups are good indicators of who is helpful in this area of finance. Ask around. Take notice of announcements in the local paper regarding simple budgeting classes. Contact the public relations department of your bank. It is surprising what they offer.

As I said, I'm a dreamer. Dreams come true when the belief and spirituality are strong. After all, wasn't this country founded on dreams? So was everything else that is powerfully positive. We can change our dysfunctional patterns regarding the money connection of credit, cash and co-dependency.

Acknowledgments

I learned a lot of my spending habits and co-dependency from my mother, who, on reflection, never stood a chance. She was the middle child of 13 children born in England to Polish immigrant parents in 1903. She was raised in the Orthodox Jewish, East-European mentality which believed if you aren't a son, you're a nobody. Some of her sisters got away from that but only by "marrying well." I told more of her story and mine in *The Child That Never Was.*

So much has come to the surface in the last several years since I went for ACoA treatment at the Caron Foundation. The program opened up so many areas of denial that set me on this path of discovery and recovery. After 10 months of aftercare with Eda Lou Higgins, "The Wonderful," I went to Dr. Jerry Judd, "The Incredible," at the Shalom Mountain, Livingstone Manor, New York. At that loving safe place I screamed out the rage of the enraged child and accelerated the recovery process.

I also learned a lot about my mother; how her feelings of low self-esteem, inferiority, guilt and shame geared her life to "doing for" everybody and anybody, including financially. As I think back on my childhood, I truly was in the dark. I knew there were arguments about money and who had the control. I heard the abuse and, oh, how I saw the submission. I knew my mother was close to some of her sisters and none of her brothers. Basically, I felt she was pitied, abused and taken for granted. Her gratitude at their attention was pathetic. I learned to be grateful in all the wrong areas. If you don't have it — "it" being whatever the others had — get it, no matter how.

My mother had a friend I called Aunt Peg. Her daughter, Jill, now living in Thornton, Ontario, has been my
friend since the age of three. Jill is my conscience in this
and my first book because she was there. Sometimes I
doubt my memory and certainly those who knew my
mother in their own way challenge me. Jill knows and she
says, "Right on, Yvonne!" "How true! How true!" It's good
to have had someone who can reinforce me during the
painful writing therapy before the recovery process.

I believe Aunt Peg was the only person my mother
trusted. I know they were able to relate to one another's
fate. Even though I know little about Peggy Ward — her
stage name, I believe — I loved her. My mother was different when Aunt Peg was around. She would stand up to
my father because Aunt Peg did. Peg wasn't afraid of him.
I know my mother's trust was well placed.

We get caught up in the negatives, the deprivation, and
the unconscionable from our past and tend to forget those
who were there for us. I had forgotten the strength, love,
courage and tenacity of Aunt Peg, who saw my mother
through a whole lot of hell and probably bailed her out
several times.

In recovery from co-dependency and money issues,
strength of character and resolve in a beloved person can
shape the future. It isn't always someone who can come
up with the money. Often that only delays the recovery
process. The person who says, "I'm here for you, no matter what," is essential. We all need somebody who is honest, confrontational, firm and resilient.

Aunt Peg provided the basis of stability for my mother.
She could turn to her for emotional support, a listening
ear and a damned good laugh. Aunt Peg had been a vaudeville dancer and her stories could curl your hair.

Here was a woman who genuinely loved my mother.
Thank you, Aunt Peg. I hope that cloud you are perched
on is solid — you're a pistol, lady! My gratitude always.

As a rule acknowledgments comprise a list of people
who have been very influential in the author's life. Mine

will be a little different. The help and encouragment I have received while compiling this book have been inestimable.

To the people who were so willing to share their time and stories, wishing to remain anonymous — thank you, thank you.

For practical, professional guidance, gratitude to:

Joy Brummell — Program director for the Red Cross Homeless Hotline — Trenton, New Jersey

Thom Murgitroyde, C.A.C., C.E.A.P. — Co-founder ACoDP — Pennsylvania

Kay Fogg — in memoriam

Marie Stilkind, Lisa Moro and Kathleen Fox — Health Communications — utterly amazing

The nameless ones who sent articles, suggestions, information and questionnaires.

My secretary, Lydia Hecker—such patience will not go unrewarded.

Yvonne Kaye

I am. Therefore I am.

Appendix

Basic Do-It-Yourself Planning Chart
(Compiled by Tony Severns)

INCOME:	WEEKLY	MONTHLY	YEARLY
Net Earnings from Job			
Investment Income			
Gifts or Inheritances			
Alimony or Child Support			
Other			
1. Total Income			
FIXED EXPENSES:			
Mortgage or Rent			
Taxes (Property, Quarterly Income)			
Debt Repayments (Loans, Installment Purchases)			
Insurance Premiums			
Alimony/Child Support			
Other			
2. Total Fixed Expenses			
3. DISPOSABLE INCOME (Line 1 less Line 2)			
FLEXIBLE EXPENSES:			
Transportation			
Charitable Contributions			

Child Care

Clothing

Education

Entertainment

Gifts

Groceries

Household
   (Furnishings,
   Repairs)

Investments

Medical

Personal Allowances

Savings — Regular

Savings — Retirement

Unreimbursed Business
   Expenses

Utilities

Vacation

Other

4. Total Flexible
   Expenses

5. Subtract Line 4
   from Line 3

If the result is zero or more, congratulations! You have a *workable budget*. However, if the result is a negative amount, you will need to re-evaluate your *flexible* spending habits and allocate a specific amount to each category.

First: Set priorities. Assign a number from 1 to 3 to each category according to its level of importance to you.

Second: Divide Line 3 by Line 4 and subtract the result from 100% to determine the percentage amount of adjustment needed. If the total difference is 20%, for example, then you must reduce your flexible expenses by a total of 20%.

Third: Start with #3 categories and reduce those by 30%. Then reduce #2 categories by 20%. Then reduce #1 categories by 10%. Keep adjusting until all categories are within agreeable, livable amounts and the total flexible expenses equal your available disposable income.

6. Revise your budget monthly for the first three months, then quarterly for the first year. After 12 months your spending habits should be healthy enough that you'll only need a checkup annually or when there is a substantial change of income or expenses.

Bibliography

Chord, Sylvia. **Engaging Children's Minds.**

Fyfield, Frances. **Not That Kind Of Place.** Pocket Books, NY, 1990.

Fishel, Ruth. **Time For Joy Daily Affirmations.** Health Communications, Deerfield Beach, FL, 1988.

Kaye, Yvonne. **The Child That Never Was.** Health Communications, Deerfield Beach, FL, 1990.

Lerner, Rokelle. **Affirmations For The Inner Child.** Health Communications, Deerfield Beach, FL, 1990.

Levy, John. **Coping With International Wealth.**

Make Your Paycheck Last. Harsand Press, WI, 1990.

Mandino, Og. **The Greatest Secret In The World.** Bantam Books, NY, 1983.

Manning, Barb. **Kids Mean Business.** Liberty Publications, FL, 1985.

Maltz, Maxwell. **Psycho-Cybernetics And Self-Fulfillment.** Bantam, NY, 1973.

McCormack, Matt. **What They Still Don't Teach You At Harvard.** Bantam Books, NY, 1989.

McGinniss, Joe. **Blind Faith.** President Press, CA, 1988.

McGinniss, Joe. **Fatal Vision.** Putnam Publishing Group, NY, 1983.

Moe, Harold and Sandy. **Teach Your Child The Value Of Money.** Harsand Press, WI, 1987.

Mundis, Jerrold. **How To Get Out Of Debt, Stay Out Of Debt And Live Prosperously.** Bantam Books, NY, 1988.

Robinson, Bryan. **Soothing Moments: Daily Meditations For Fast-Track Living.** Health Communications, Deerfield Beach, FL, 1990.

Schaef, Anne Wilson. **Meditations For Women Who Do Too Much.** Harper and Row, NY, 1990.

Smith, Ann. **Overcoming Perfectionism.** Health Communications, Deerfield Beach, FL, 1990.

Somers, Suzanne. **Keeping Secrets.** Warner Books, NY, 1988.

Touchstones: A Book Of Daily Meditations For Men. Hazelden, MN, 1986.

Weinstein, Grace, W. **Children And Money: A Parent's Guide.** Signet Books, NY, 1985.

Educational Materials And Resources:

Classroom Guide to Money
Money Education Program
10 North Main St.
Yardley, PA 19067

Public Information Department
Federal Reserve Bank of New York
33 Liberty St.
New York, NY 10045
Comic Book Series: *The Story of Money, The Story of Banks, The Story of Consumer Credit,* which include a lot of additional referral sources.

Fidelity Investments
You and Your Money: A Learning Unit for Children

Penny Power
Consumers Union
P.O. Box 51777
Boulder, CO 80321

Young Americans' Bank
250 Steele St.
Denver, CO 80206

Daily Affirmation Books from . . .
Health Communications

GENTLE REMINDERS FOR CO-DEPENDENTS: Daily Affirmations
Mitzi Chandler

With insight and humor, Mitzi Chandler takes the co-dependent and the
adult child through the year. Gentle Reminders is for those in recovery
who seek to enjoy the miracle each day brings.

ISBN 1-55874-020-1 $6.95

TIME FOR JOY: Daily Affirmations
Ruth Fishel

With quotations, thoughts and healing energizing affirmations these daily
messages address the fears and imperfections of being human, guiding us
through self-acceptance to a tangible peace and the place within where
there is *time for joy.*

ISBN 0-932194-82-6 $6.95

AFFIRMATIONS FOR THE INNER CHILD
Rokelle Lerner

This book contains powerful messages and helpful suggestions aimed at
adults who have unfinished childhood issues. By reading it daily we can
end the cycle of suffering and move from pain into recovery.

ISBN 1-55874-045-6 $6.95

DAILY AFFIRMATIONS: For Adult Children of Alcoholics
Rokelle Lerner

Affirmations are a way to discover personal awareness, growth and
spiritual potential, and self-regard. Reading this book gives us an
opportunity to nurture ourselves, learn who we are and what we want
to become.

ISBN 0-932194-47-3
(Little Red Book) $6.95
(New Cover Edition) $6.95

SOOTHING MOMENTS: Daily Meditations For Fast-Track Living
Bryan E. Robinson, Ph.D.

This is designed for those leading fast-paced and high-pressured lives
who need time out each day to bring self-renewal, joy and serenity into
their lives.

ISBN 1-55874-075-9 $6.95

3201 S.W. 15th Street,
Deerfield Beach, FL 33442-8190
1-800-851-9100

Health
Communications, Inc.

Other Books By . . .
Health Communications

ADULT CHILDREN OF ALCOHOLICS
Janet Woititz
Over a year on *The New York Times* Best-Seller list, this book is the primer on Adult Children of Alcoholics.
ISBN 0-932194-15-X $6.95

STRUGGLE FOR INTIMACY
Janet Woititz
Another best-seller, this book gives insightful advice on learning to love more fully.
ISBN 0-932194-25-7 $6.95

BRADSHAW ON: THE FAMILY: A Revolutionary Way of Self-Discovery
John Bradshaw
The host of the nationally televised series of the same name shows us how families can be healed and individuals can realize full potential.
ISBN 0-932194-54-0 $9.95

HEALING THE SHAME THAT BINDS YOU
John Bradshaw
This important book shows how toxic shame is the core problem in our compulsions and offers new techniques of recovery vital to all of us.
ISBN 0-932194-86-9 $9.95

HEALING THE CHILD WITHIN: Discovery and Recovery for
Adult Children of Dysfunctional Families — Charles Whitfield, M.D.
Dr. Whitfield defines, describes and discovers how we can reach our Child Within to heal and nurture our woundedness.
ISBN 0-932194-40-0 $8.95

A GIFT TO MYSELF: A Personal Guide To Healing My Child Within
Charles L. Whitfield, M.D.
Dr. Whitfield provides practical guidelines and methods to work through the pain and confusion of being an Adult Child of a dysfunctional family.
ISBN 1-55874-042-2 $11.95

HEALING TOGETHER: A Guide To Intimacy And Recovery For
Co-dependent Couples — Wayne Kritsberg, M.A.
This is a practical book that tells the reader why he or she gets into dysfunctional and painful relationships, and then gives a concrete course of action on how to move the relationship toward health.
ISBN 1-55784-053-8 $8.95

3201 S.W. 15th Street,
Deerfield Beach, FL 33442-8190
1-800-851-9100

Health Communications, Inc.